STARS THROUGH THE CLOUDS

The Collected Poetry of Donald T. Williams

R. A. Forrest Scholar and Professor Emeritus,
Toccoa Falls College,
Toccoa Falls, GA

2nd Edition, Expanded and Revised

Lantern Hollow Press

Toccoa, GA

Cover Design: Kami Melton
Stars on cover and photo for Book 5: Michael Covington
Interior formatting: Brian Melton and Katherine Jones

Taliessin line drawings by Ruby Dunlap, used by permission.
Interior photography by Brian Melton, all rights reserved.

Library of Congress Control Number: 2020903651

Williams, Donald T., 1951-
Stars Through the Clouds: The Collected Poetry of Donald T. Williams
/ Donald T. Williams
Includes bibliographic references and indexes.

Summary: **Stars through the Clouds** *tries to restore poetry to the
writing of poetry. It is a record of the glimpses of truth, goodness, and
beauty the author has been granted and his efforts to bring them into
focus.*

ISBN-13: 978-1-7328680-0-7

1. *Poetry.* 2. *Christianity in Literature*

Though here at journey's end I lie
In darkness buried deep,
Beyond all towers strong and high,
Beyond all mountains steep,

Above all shadows rides the Sun
And Stars forever dwell.
I will not say the day is done,
Nor bid the Stars farewell.

Sam Gamgee
The Return of the King

ᔍ Table of Contents ᔊ

iv

ᘓ Foreword ᙏ

In a college literature class I was once teaching, we read a bit of terse, sparse free verse by a noted American writer who specialized in the sort of misery-bathed literary confession that makes one wonder if Freud might have done us more of a favor not to have invented Psychology. A student looked up and asked, "What, besides the fact that it ends halfway across the page, makes this a poem?" The student was a fairly serious, mature student taking night classes and working on a degree in business. Rather than dismiss his question, I think we need to understand the wisdom in it from the perspective of disciplines outside of literature. English professors cannot agree on a precise definition of poetry, but the student's question is absolutely valid: If it does not employ any poetic devices other than splitting lines at half page, in what sense is it poetry? It has insight? So does prose. It has a kind of artistic freedom with the spacing of lines on the page? So does contemporary prose. It evokes a real and gritty emotion? So does prose.

My answer to the student was "Welcome to Postmodernism." A simple definition of Postmodernism is the state of art and literature since the end of the Second World War. Postmodernism, like poetry, eludes an agreed-upon definition, but for a different reason. Postmodernism cannot be defined because it is the rejection of definition, of boundaries, of the very possibility of identity or objective existence. The perfect movie-moment definition of Postmodernism comes in the Beatles' movie *Yellow Submarine*, when a large Peter Max monster with a trumpet-shaped snout, known simply as "the Vacuum Cleaner Monster," sucks up all the sea animals in its vicinity. It then proceeds to suck up the sea and the sea floor, and, finding itself on a sheet of featureless white, discovers its own tail, sucks that up, and vanishes.

In short, when it comes to literature, when we have cast off all definitions and all traditions and the mentally ill drivel of some pre-suicidal case in New York City, neatly split by the printer at half page, is the best and brightest of our new poetic lights, then there is simply no way forward. Poetry itself becomes something to be questioned and, as satirists find when they practice a no-holds-barred approach to their satire, one soon saws off the limb one is sitting on and falls into silence. Postmodernism is a cliff edge with a wooden roadblock bearing the sign, "Danger. No way forward." If one is not standing on something, one is falling endlessly in the abyss.

Into this scene comes Donald T. Williams. He is no weighty professor from Harvard or Yale, ruminating over the questions of Postmodernism and the Modernism which gave it birth in weighty journals that rock the halls of the Modern Language Association. He is more of a Muir or a Thoreau, teaching at a small college in the Georgia mountains. This volume of his poetry is not likely to make the New York Times bestseller list any time soon. But as Dr. Johnson knew, the readers of the future, not us, will pass the final judgment on a poet's efforts. Like Thoreau, Williams is far more concerned with the real weight of experience in this beautiful planet's wild places and also its daily scenes, with the spiritual reality that echoes from that creation, and with the poets who came before us and knew with certainty these great Realities before literary fashion swept them aside. Williams is calling to us to softly remind us of a simple and common-sense truth that all of us know instinctively: When there's no way forward, the sensible thing to do is turn around and walk back the way one came.

Williams is startling and revolutionary in clearly setting forth the simple, lightning-bolt realization that all the "illusions" that were swept away after the first world war in thought and in poetry were not in fact illusions at all, but rather very real truths that couldn't be faced in the light of what was perceived as the failure of civilization. Humanity had not perfected itself and the horror show of the trenches across France proved it. Yet the simpler and truer answer, that we were in need of grace, was out of fashion, and so the great cultural yard sale (everything must go!) of Modernism occurred. Williams not only reminds us that grace is freely given but that all of creation sings that song as part of its praises.

And Williams has returned poetry to the writing of poetry. Poetic devices create verse. Here you will find all the great forms that graced English verse for centuries with new life breathed into them. Owen Barfield went further and insisted that poetry, in order to be more than doggerel or indifferent verse, must cause the reader to undergo a "felt change of consciousness." Perhaps that is rather a tall order, but if so, Don Williams achieves it here with deceptively artless ease. Someone once said of reading the work of C.S. Lewis that it "caused one to grow in sanity." I find very few other authors of whom that may be said: J. R. R. Tolkien, Madeleine L'Engle, Robert Frost, and not many more. But it can be said of the poetry of Donald Williams.

Williams is not likely to get a call any time soon to go work at Harvard and lead a poetic revolution. Nor is this little book likely to make the *New York Times* bestseller list. But then, doing something large and showy is not his gift. He is another incarnation of that spirit of Thoreau which quietly calls for an inner revolution which can only take place in the quiet woods of one's own heart. If this book ever becomes a bestseller, then, it will be because people passed it hand to hand and could not bear not to speak of it. So let it begin. I invite the reader to turn these pages and take a walk through these poetic woods, and to grow in sanity.

James Prothero
San Juan Capistrano
Christmas Day 2009

℘ Introduction ℘

The book that you hold in your hands is my life's work.

You might not think so from looking at my resume. I have published ten other books, many articles, countless reviews, and (if you count my website) numerous sermons, all in prose. I have appeared before the world, both in the flesh and in print, as a College Professor, a Literary Historian, a Preacher, a Bible Teacher, a Missionary, a Musician, a Culture Critic, an Apologist, and maybe even as a bit of a Theologian. I still believe in almost everything I have ever said in all of those roles, and I would jump at the chance to say it again—even in prose. I believe it was all worth living for, and much of it worth dying for. Yet if I were limited to what I have said outside of this volume, I would feel that my life was incomplete, indeed, that I had been a poor steward of my gifts and failed to do the main thing I was put on this planet to do.

Which was to write this book.

How can I say that? It is easy to get the impression that nobody cares about poetry anymore. And it certainly seems that to hang your hat on that hook these days is to condemn yourself to a well-deserved obscurity, not to mention irrelevance. Now, that's what most people would call a squandering of one's gifts and opportunities! Some people painfully close to me have called it that. I understand. So be it. Nevertheless . . .

Nevertheless, I stick to my guns. If I have had anything significant to contribute, it is here. If I have been enabled to say anything worth hearing about the meaning of a passage of Scripture or of a work of literature or of life, it is here. If I have ever succeeded in clarifying an argument or perceiving the significance of a bit of evidence, it is here. If I have been granted any valuable insight into the pathos of the human condition or the love of God or the power of the Gospel, it is here. If I have been granted any clear vision of the Truth of things, the Goodness of God, or the Beauty of Nature or Christ, it is here. Here! So what was I doing before?

I tried to say some of it in prose because that was what I was able to publish in today's book market. And I am grateful for that opportunity. One does what one can. But my most profound meditations on all these things, in their most powerful expression, for whatever they may be worth, are here: in the poems. That is what poetry is for. That is what real poetry—if I have ever been granted to achieve it—is.

If these poems can re-convince anyone of that most forgotten of truths, so that he or she may be brought to see a little more clearly the even greater Truths which are their subject matter, I shall not have lived in vain.

Donald T. Williams, PhD

Toccoa, GA., January 30, 2010;

Revised, April 2, 2018

ഌ Preface to the Second Edition ଔ

My poetic production has slowed down as I move through my sixties. Partly it is because I have become more skeptical of my own work, remembering how many other poets spent their declining years doing cheap imitations of their earlier selves and wishing to avoid that fate. Partly it is because after fifty-plus years of observing nature, people, and books, thinking about what I have seen in them, and trying to make the responses they seemed to demand of me, I find myself, like many of the old, in danger of repeating myself. After a walk or a book I will start a new poem and then realize, "I've already said that. I've already expressed that idea, already used that metaphor. There is nothing really new here." I think it is incumbent on us to hush when that happens. Sometimes, I am able to do so.

Nevertheless, I still occasionally manage to write a poem that I think is worth keeping. There are more than twenty new pieces in this edition, scattered in the places where they logically seemed to fit. I have also corrected some errors in the first edition and provided a complete table of contents and indices of first lines and titles.

I made some pretty grandiose claims in the Introduction I wrote eight years ago. Well, they were not so much claims as aspirations. I still have them. If I have even gotten close a few times, there may be something here of value for you to find. You do an old man a great favor by looking to see.

Donald T. Williams, PhD
Toccoa, GA
November 6, 2019

ജ Book I ര

Times Around the Southern Appalachians

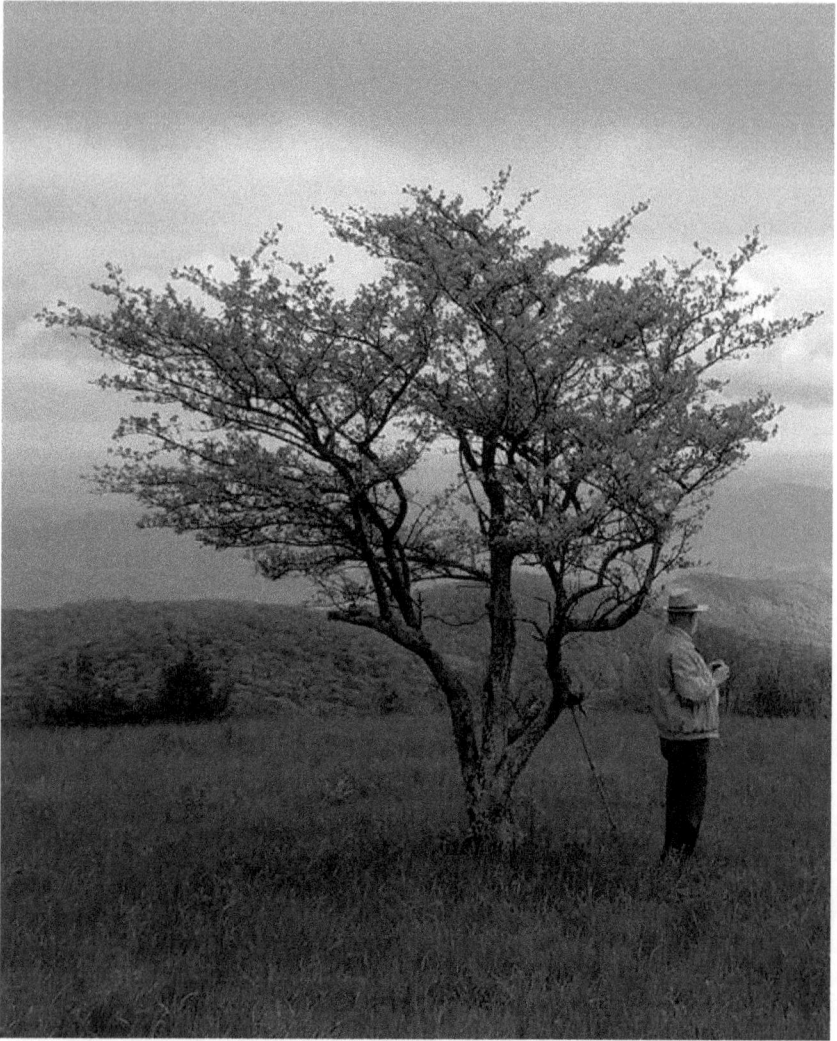

The author surveys the Appalachian Mountains
from Cole Mountain Meadow,
Nelson County, Virginia

℘ PROLOGUE: ℘
The Sense of Place

This is a book about certain people, places, and times, and their significance. Most of the places are to be found in the Appalachian mountains of Georgia and North Carolina or the Piedmont, the foothills descending from them to the coastal plain. The few that are not a part of that landscape are seen through eyes that were raised in places that are. Most of the people and all of the times are no longer to be found anywhere in this world, unless in these pages.

For there is no place that does not change with time. But some there should be that change more slowly than others, so slowly that the change embodies a pattern, becomes itself a continual going back. It is a sign of our need for such places that going back is what we too are continually trying to do. A man is fortunate if, in a lifetime, he finds a few places which allow him, in some measure, to succeed. Their shapes will haunt his heart and mold his life between his visits; and visit them again you may be sure he will, in his imagination if he is not allowed to return in the flesh.

There is no sufficient name for what they call him back to. It cannot be that the shape of a tree against the sky, the stillness of a hill-encircled lake, the taste of spring water flowing from a rock that Moses might just have struck with his staff, the flash of a deer's rump or the rush of quail, or the sounds of surf and seagull are really the quarry he is after, though in themselves they are certainly things one would not wish to lose. If the hunter were after the deer, he would rest once it was in his freezer; but he does not. The deer is only a seasonal embodiment of something he never will attain. He himself may be only dimly aware of this mystery and its influence on his life. But he instinctively knows it is better to seek in the deer and not to find than, staying at home, never to seek at all. He knows that, whether he himself should go or not, if there were no deer to hunt when the leaves begin to fly, life would become an empty husk. He acts on that instinctive knowledge in a yearly ritual, and, sitting in his blind, comes back to something faintly akin to sight.

It is no use to ask him what he sees. He could not tell you if he tried, and might not even understand the question. Indeed he does not properly see anything at all; but so far as he can be said to see during the rest of the year, it is the vision in the blind that he sees by. The blind, the unseen deer whose presence is felt even if it does not come, the silence and the blowing leaves, the wind and the cold, the feel of polished wood and blue steel, the cramping in the legs, define a place. It is a place which a man occupies, even for the first time, as one who has been there before and who therefore returns, comes back, in search of something vaguely felt as lost.

A man does not stand in such a place to find what he has lost, but to be reminded that he has lost it. His heart tells him that, if his daily life is the wholeness he was made for, then something is wrong that cannot be put right: If all is swept away by time and lost, it matters little what is swept away. And so he needs to keep coming back to something which reminds him of his woeful brokenness, thereby to be kept from the despair of health. For a man who is diseased may without contradiction hope to be cured, even if only a miracle could do it.

There is a meadow at the feet of Standing Indian in North Carolina. There are stars shining above a village without electricity in the Andes of Colombia. There is a bowl between the peaks of Pinchincha in Ecuador, surrounded by crags and silence. There is a series of dunes on a beach in Virginia that suddenly gives way to the sea. There is a lake and a pier and a tall spruce in the hills of northern Georgia. There is a spring thick with yellow leaves where deer come to drink at the first light of dawn. There is a path, one of many, always winding further into the forest.

I know that these places exist and that time has not yet swept them away. In some I have stood many times, in some but once. My memories of some are recorded in this book. In each I have relaxed, for a moment, and realized in that release how hard I had been straining, leaning against the current, how sore my muscles had become. In none of them is the undertow quite absent; yet for a while they are places in which a man can stand, for a moment, without fear of being swept away--and thus images, perhaps, of a place beyond the world where he can take his stand forever.

Toccoa, Georgia

Fall, 2009

Times in the Appalachian High Country

There is a time for walking and breathing hard
From the work of pushing ancient mountains down
Until they stand beneath your weary feet.
There is the time for stopping to wipe the fog
From off your glasses so you can see more fog,
The dim walls on your left, and on your right
The sun-bright moving shadows of the mist.
There is the time when unexpectedly
The wind whips 'round a corner, and the fog
Cowers before it, breaks its ranks, and runs,
Falls back, regroups, and thus becomes a cloud,
Leaving the sun unchallenged in its claim
To rule the island peaks. There is a time
For stopping to drink from the last spring that runs
Before there is no mountain left to gather
The moisture from the sky and send it down
To fill the running stream-beds far below.
There is the time you say, "This is the top."
But you will say that several times before
There's finally nowhere left to go but down.
But it seems false to say there is a time
For standing all alone upon the peak,
Not under, now, so much as in the sky.
It makes no difference that your watch-hand still
Moves like it always has. If this is time,
It is a time that's like no other time.
The watch ticks on, but leaves us far behind,
Which is why we catch up to it with a jerk
And barely can get back to camp by nightfall.
Is it because they've seen so much of time
That they can almost lift us out of it--

Does it grow thinner, flowing o'er their backs
The way the wind does, so there's less of it
To shield us from the blazing depths of heaven--
Have they seen something through it that we haven't?
The mountains will remain when we have gone
Back down beneath the clouds, but we will take
Our glimpses of the mystery back with us
To prod us into poems or metaphysics
Or merely silent thinking by the fire.
Meanwhile, the stones are silent in the starlight
Until there is a time we can return.

℘ Part I ℘
The Passing Seasons

Tempus Fugit

From green to brown to white and back to green,
　　Earth changed her wardrobe as the seasons passed:
　　Always the dresser, whether she was seen
　　In summer's heat or in the winter's blast.
The moon that sailed the sky a thin canoe
　　Swelled to a richly laden argosy,
　　Discharged her cargo, disappeared from view,
　　And then began again her odyssey.
A strong young man who has a race to run
　　And charges up the mountain of the sky:
　　That is how we first perceive the sun,
　　'Til down the other side he falls to die.
So many cycles, yet it still seems strange,
　　Such continuity in so much change.

Vernal Equinox
March, 2004

"Look at me! I'm blue! I'm blue!"
     "Look at me! I'm red!"
That is what the Bluebird trilled
     And the Cardinal said.

"Look at me! I am the sign
     That Spring is on the way."
That is what I clearly heard
     The early Robin say.

"Look at us! We're brightest yellow!
     We were the first who came!"
Thus the quickly blooming Jonquils
     Also made their claim.

"Look at me! I am the cause
     That Spring is near at hand."
The earlier-rising Sun was sure
     That I would understand.

Now, to ignore such urgent carols
     Surely would be rude,
As it would be illogical
     If one did not conclude

That Winter soon must take the hint
     That he did not belong
And go off in a huff to let them
     Sing their gentle song.

A Poem for Pentecost Sunday (1975)

There is in Nature a strange ability
Given to the first young leaves in Springtime
To catch and hold the golden, streaming sunlight
And slowly release it back into the morning.
Each then becomes a burning tongue of fire,
Glowing green with oak or elm impatience
To get on with its summer occupation
Of turning into tree the soil and water
Sent up by roots, those ever-stretching branches
That search as far beneath the earth for water
As those above seek in the air for sunlight.
These flame-tongued leaves are also tongues for
      speaking.
Are they moved by, or do they move the breezes
That fan out, gently heralding the Springtime?
At any rate, 'tis sure they pass the message.
From South to North, from tree to tree, they whisper,
"Awaken, for the Spring is surely coming!"
And slowly northward, like a swelling sea-wave,
Rippling flows the glad rebirth of Nature.
God made her thus; so 'twas no accident
That first by tongues of fire the message spread
That *man* could be reborn—that Death was dead.

Birth of a Squash Plant

In hurricane or earthquake, Nature's power
Is less seen than when newborn leaves uncoil:
A thousand cells dividing every hour,
Their seeming effortlessness cloaking toil--
God's glory pushes upward through the soil,

And pushes on, in ever-creeping lines
And swelling gourds, with sweetness to be filled
By Time, and Rain, and Sunlight, and the Vine's
Inscrutable photosynthesizing skill--
The glory of God spreads out around the hill.

Weather Report
Delivered by Radagast the Brown
To the People of Harlindon
March, S. R. 1420

What news does the West Wind bring today
From lands undying, far away?

Joy she brings from Westernesse
And comes with ocean waves cavorting,
While tall clouds in gallant dress
Ride on her back to watch the sporting.
    Reaching the land
    With no less than
A thousand thunder-voices snorting,
    She laughs with glee;
    Nor hill nor tree
Will be her headlong passage thwarting.

(Blowing leaves and blowing paper
With the West Wind dance and caper.)

Spring Metaphor

The breeze, a fickle partner in the dance,
      Proceeds from leaf to leaf: "May I cut in?"
      He whirls them 'round, 'til, giddy with romance,
      He then moves on to where he has not been.
The leaves, left fluttering like human hearts,
      Return but slowly to serenity,
      Whereon another suitor's airy arts
      Stir them again to hope, most cruelly.
They'll have no lasting peace until they lie
      Beneath a blanket of the bitter snow,
      For, dallying thus, then lightly passing by,
      The teasing breezes never cease to blow.
But men have minds to understand their lot.
      You'd think that it would help, but it does not.

May Morning

I find myself increasingly in favor of this weather,
Glad that there should be such things as billowing pecan
      trees,
That every leaf should wildly dance in the wind with gay
      abandon
While the dark and somber pine trees pretend to take no
      notice
But the bright, elfin sun-beams dart about and take in
      everything,
Especially the diamonds bestowed upon the grass
By the largesse of the thunderstorm that lately rumbled
      past.

The Drought of '86: July

Fifteen feet of barrel-floated dock
Lie beached, a grotesque whale upon the shore;
And you could walk another ten or more
Before you hit the water. Many a rock
That men's eyes have not seen since back before
The dam was built lies drying in the sun.
Already autumn yellow has begun
To show up in the limbs and on the floor
As trees go dormant, trying, one by one,
To save themselves to grow another day.
Fish die; the corn is dead; the people pray,
But not yet seriously enough to shun
The wide gate and the broad and easy way.

A Premonition

The first faint hint that Fall is coming soon
(It's early in the evening that you mostly feel it,
Or early morning--for the sun by noon
Will be reminding you that it's still summer)
Is not the leaves. Much as they were in June,
You still can see them in their best green raiment.
A barely perceptible sharpness in the moon,
An unexplained desire to breathe more deeply,
An unheard modulation in the tune
The wind sings on its way down from the mountains--
Not singly, but yet somehow in their blending,
They whisper of another Summer's ending.

Reds

Red: flash of cardinal, barely seen;
    Red: leaves of maple, flecked with flame;
    Red: dogwood berries (leaves still green);
    Red: other leaves without a name;
Red: mountain apples, cheap to buy;
    Red: candy apples at the fair;
    Red: clouds across the evening sky;
    Red: children's cheeks in frosty air;
Red: sumac's multi-fingered hand;
    Red: as always, by the road, the clay;
    Red: flannel pajamas, sooner than planned;
    Red: flames on hearth at close of day.
Red: different shades and hues, but all
    Read: Glory of a Georgia fall.

Ode to a Shirt

I could never wear this shirt in summer;
Winter, spring, were just as bad.
This is a shirt for wearing in autumn,
Full with autumn colors, plaid.

Bright, the glory of the leaf-host,
Brown, the wind-blown stalk of corn,
Chill, the frost on pumpkin orange
Seen while walking, early morn.

The spirits of these things lie sleeping,
Woven deep among the threads.
Tomorrow will be time for wearing;
Summer will at last have fled.

I could never wear this shirt in summer;
Winter, spring were just as bad.
This is a shirt for wearing in autumn,
Full with autumn colors, plaid.

November

Underfoot, the leaves are damp and cold
    Which yesterday were dancing with the breeze
    In flashing pirouettes of red and gold
    Set loose from still abundant canopies.
But now the bare-boned outlines of the trees
    Are etched in black across a slate-gray sky.
    The wind feels like the prelude to a freeze;
    It may bring sleet when next it passes by.
It's not the first time leaves have had to die:
    The wind has sung their funeral dirge before,
    But now it seems like every year that cry
    Comes sooner and we seem to feel it more;
For every cycle has a single thrust:
    What's born of earth must soon return to dust.

Autumn Ritual

A ceaseless movement, hub and rim and spoke:
    The colors turn in endless cycles 'round
    From gold to green, to yellow or red, to brown
On birch and chestnut, maple, elm, and oak.
Although the mists of time their movements cloak,
    They do not rest for long upon the ground:
    From earth, to roots, to branches; then, back down
They dance through air, or up again in smoke.

So what becomes of those we pile and burn?
    Trees owe the gods a tithe of what they make;
    We send the offering up for them with rake
And match, ensuring that the wheel will turn
    Once more from gold to green, to red, to brown,
    From earth, to roots, to branches, then back down.

Vision

It was a deep, dark forest. No wind stirred
  The woven branches there. No greater sound
  In all that heavy stillness could be heard
  Than worn-out oak leaves dropping to the ground.
The floor was covered with their rusty brown
  As I, not unaffected by the gloom,
  Came slowly shuffling through with eyes cast
      down.
  The arching branches, closing in, assumed
The aspect of dim vaults in ancient tombs,
  When, sudden, splashed amidst the brown, a small
  Bright patch of gold I saw, the earth in bloom,
  Where one lone maple'd let her leaf-cloak fall.
Tell me: was it leaves I saw that hour,
  Or Zeus descending in a golden shower?

Leaves

  If there were clouds in the sky
  They would show the speed of the wind
  By racing each other westward,
  Ne'er to be seen again

  But the heavens are empty today,
  So we'll have to settle for leaves
  In a reckless, cross-country scramble,
  Trying to outrun the breeze.

November, 1970

I stand on the knife-edge 'twixt Autumn and Winter
And watch the spent leaves blow.
To remember is to be
And to love, to know—
          And so—
The leaves are turned to snow.

Winter in Illinois
A Georgian's Chronicle

I

The corn-stalk brown looked almost white
Beside the black limbs of the trees:
A bleak etude in dark and light,
A prelude to the coming night
When endless miles of deep, soft white
Are all the wanderer sees.

II

        Freezing rain,
        Tree's bane.
        Can you hear it falling?
        Coming down
        With the sound
        Of the cracking
        And the snapping
        Of the pain
        In the branches
        Of the trees!

III

See fast, how the snowflakes floating fly,
With a tumble-down, wind -whipped hurry, pass by,
Blown from their homes in the sullen sky,
Seeking new nests in the grass.

IV

See how the snow-fall, the silver shadow,
Lies like a blanket upon the low land,
Marches in waves through the fields and the meadows,
Falls soft in the forest, where tree-folk stand.
Molded in strange shapes, it clings to the bridges,
Twisted and tortured and carved by the wind;
Piled high, it silently smothers the city,
And a rest from the meaningless hurry of Men
(Who, knowing not whither nor why they must go,
Spend all their time running, first to and then fro)
Is the present of peace we receive from the snow.

V

It's April now, but you would never know,
To watch the stubborn falling of the snow.
Except to show that Winter has its nerve,
I cannot see what purpose it could serve,
This cruel encroachment on the rights of Spring.
In Georgia, we would never let the thing
Get near this far; there, as in Camelot,
The Winter never stays where it should not.
But here it doesn't have the sense to know
When its welcome's gone, and it should go.

Commentary, Rom. 8:22

And the Sea rises and falls, and the Moon walks,
And the Leaves unfold like a scroll rolled each Spring,
But no one stops to read them, and the Wind talks
Of the flesh that weeps and the soul that cannot sing.

And the Sun rises and sets, and the Rain falls,
And the Leaves achieve a glory of red and gold,
But the long Darkness grows, and the Snow calls,
And the Leaves clutch like withered hands, and old.

And the Crone counts the dead hands in the dark light
And will not tell the numbers that she finds.
And if the Child can be born in the hard Night,
He's swaddled in the subtle shroud she winds.

And the Sea rises and falls, and the Moon walks,
And the Leaves unfold like a scroll rolled each Spring,
But no one stops to read them, and the Wind talks
Of the flesh that weeps and the soul that cannot sing.

To Concentrate the Mind: December Walk

Ambling flight of crow
Across the winter sky
Makes me think of coming snow.
        I wonder why?

Vigilance of hawk
Upon a power line:
Bad news for the mouse he stalks
        With single mind.

Chattering of jay
From branch of rippling pine:
The wind blows his thoughts away
        Like mine.

Fluttering of sparrow
Along a wire fence;
Behind him, like a piercing arrow,
        The hawk descends.

January, 1971

That cloud . . .
And that horizon . . .
And those trees . . .
Arranged in just that way
That I now see
Give just the very faintest ray
Of hope that this long winter may
Indeed, at long, long last, give way
To spring.

"Spring" in the Upper Midwest

Forty degrees and gray and misting rain,
The sunrise just a lessening of gloom
(You'd hardly call it light) to say that Time
Had not yet wholly failed in its refrain.
Back home the dogwood trees would be in bloom;
Here snowdrifts linger, crusted o'er with grime.
So ends the pure white promise of December:
In April slush and mud it meets its doom--
And we can't seem to make ourselves remember
Another season or another clime.
We know there once was sunlight; we assume
Somewhere above the clouds, in joy sublime,
It reigns. But we need faith to fan the embers
Of hope here in this dank and dismal tomb.

A Suite for Five Seasons

Summer

"Et inquietum est cor nostrum . . ."
Luxuriant, green-growth leaves that tower tall
    Above our heads to form a mighty ceiling
    Are surely destined down to die and fall,
    The bare, left lifeless, lifted limbs revealing
That bore them up until the fatal voice
    Of Frost should come and whisper softly, sealing
    Their fate. They choose (and yet, they have no
        choice)
    To go a-wandering, homeless vagabonds,
Seeking for a reason to rejoice
    More than they had when, high, in soft green
        fronds,
    They formed a restful, rustling canopy
    To filter sunlight into summer ponds.
And I wonder why men (and I am one) must be
    So like the leaves they see on every tree.

Fall

"Omnes enim peccaverunt, et egent gloria Dei."
The leaves so choked the pool they made a floor
    You'd almost think a man could walk across.
    And if they weren't enough, the wind drove more
    In right on top of them, until the moss
Was all that was left clinging to the trees.
    A few short months the proud, green host had stood
    On high. Now at the mercy of the breeze
    They were shaken down and scattered through the wood,

Unable to find another resting place
      Unless they were caught by the stagnant ponds
      Which stood around the sun-forsaken waste
      Enticing the outcasts to embrace new bonds.
And one could wish the leaves would tell which curse,
      Autonomy or slavery, is the worse.

Yule

"Vidimus enim stellam eius in oriente,
et venimus adorare eium."
The concrete walks were softer than the ground.
      The pond was smooth and hard, though scarred by skates.
      A few lone futile flakes of snow whirled 'round
      In the iron grip of a wind that howled with hate.
The skaters that had scarred the pond were gone,
      And rested now, no doubt, by warm hearth-fires.
      They'd left the wind to prowl the waste alone
      And wail of its own alien desires.
At times, through scudding clouds, a star would flame,
      Hinting from a height remote and pure
      Of longings of its own it could not name,
      Though still, the message came, and that was sure.
But once, they say, three wise men from afar
      Bowed to the Name beneath just such a star.

Winter

"Infelix ego homo, quis me liberabit,
de corpore mortis huius?"
The sky was huddled up next to the ground
      As if for mutual warmth against the cold.
      But that there was no warmth there to be found
      Was plain: the earth looked hoar with frost, and
         old.

The wild wind with great pleasure swept the land
    As though constricted by the lowering sky,
    And with many a powerful, grasping, unseen hand
    Stripped naked all the trees as it passed by
And laid their twisted, inner natures bare.
    They bent beneath the wind as if with shame,
    Or some great load of lostness or despair,
    Or even greater burdens with no name.
On a day like that, no man should e'er be out;
    But out I was, and that I could not doubt.

Spring

"... donec requiescat in te."

Today is a day for praising the sun in the meadow
    And the high wind, the sky wind that's blown from
        snown peaks to our faces;
    A day for swift-gliding races of cloud-cast shadow,
    For leaf-wing, bird, all things that move to be put
        through their paces;
A day for the laughter of maidens, the giving of graces;
    A day for the splashing of singing-stream, rock-
        tumble water,
    And the blooming of sweet mountain laurel in
        seldom-seen places;
    A day for hot sun in the desert to shine even hotter,
A day for clay cliffs to be shaped by the wind-handed
    potter;
    Today is a day for the thunder and lightning to
        battle
    And roar in high passes until the great stone-
        boulders totter,
    And send down the swift-ending rain while the
        storm windows rattle;

It's a day for singing, for telling the oft-told story,
    For praising the ancient twy-natured enfleshment
        of glory.

Moment

The snow shone bright on the mountain peaks high,
And the wind blew fresh from a pale, blue sky,
And the sun smiled down on her friend the ground
    Where I did lie.

೫ Part II ೪
The Quality of Light

One of the Functions of Morning

When the first fingers of light steal through the grass,
Angling down through the spaces between the limbs
Of trees, greeting the ground-fog as they pass,
They separate the darkness into shadows
Which stretch out lengthwise clear across the meadows.
I have been up a time or two, on whims,
Early enough to see it come to pass.

For it is shy, this light that flits and skims
And touches everything so very lightly.
As imperceptibly as starlight dims
It fades to greater brightness, slips away
Before the bolder light that's merely day,
And leaves the lucky ones it touches slightly
More inclined to follow after whims.

Impression

It is Thursday again.
The world's head is bowed
By the weight of a cloud,
And gently, gently falls the rain.

Riddle

At times a window bright and clear as glass,
At times a veil of mist drawn o'er the glades,
    But always there;
Night be-jeweller of fern and grass,
Home of light and leaf and subtle shades
    Beyond compare;
Cool and wet; a hint of sassafras;
A little thin upon the upward grades,
    But sweet and fair;
Carrier over valley, peak, and pass
Of haunting melodies that stab like blades
From dulcimer or stream, erasing care:
    Mountain air.

Plane Flight

Glorious, soaring, skyscape cloud most-mountains
Have sunlight waterfalls fair and sunlight fountains.
And there between the parting light-rays, starting,
The metal-feathered silver bird comes darting
With shining, sing-wing silver sunlight flashing
And fire-tail, deep-throat voices thunder crashing.
And Earth sees just a still speck in the sky,
But those inside see eagle roads flash by
And know with eagles what it means to fly.

The Contribution of Lesser Lights

For a while he could almost count them as they came
    Like scouts, but then the whole vast army stepped
    At once into the sky and into flame.
    Like a poem he could not understand, they kept
A vigil in his spirit while he slept
    And swift were vanishing when he awoke;
    But the more glaring light of day that swept
    Them from the sky swept no soul's darkness, spoke
No lightning lines, no secrets could uncloak.
    Oh, it shone bright and clear, there was no doubt,
    And glanced gold fire from off the dull-leaved oak.
    But though man has it in him to blot out
The sun, these lesser lights still often find
    The chinks in the dark armor of his mind.

A Question for Modern Men

Every year the forest rains its leaves,
    And sleeps, and then starts over on a new
    Springtime wardrobe. Every day the dew
Catches sunlight, cufflinks on the sleeves
Of green along the arms that hold the eaves
    Of the wood aloft. Every hour the hue,
    Leaf-green, brown trunk, or shadowed depths of blue,
Re-blends and shifts with light that each receives.

And whence is all this growth and all this change
    Within such stubborn permanence of place?
    Where every seed and leaf alights by chance,
What Virtue has the potence to arrange
    The whole with such inevitable grace
    And cadence Chaos into such a dance?

The University of Georgia, North Campus, Spring 1980: The Ninth Sphere Reflected in the First

"This mist just barely lets the moonlight through.
We'll see no stars tonight."
                              "But where the moon
Is shining, you can bet the stars are too.
No matter we can't see them in this noon
Of silver foglight, for tonight the trees
Are all intent on standing in for them:
New dogwood blossoms, ranked in galaxies
And constellations, glow on every limb.
Somehow they gather in the diffuse light
And give it back in concentrated flares
Of brilliance, making dark the softer white."

"What strange astronomy is this, that dares
Set stars ablaze so far from their own sphere?"

"Well, one that knows how much we need their light,
And feels their unseen influence down here,
And, having seen them once in their full height,
Thereafter walks by faith, and not by sight."

Commentary, Job 38:7

The Novas were the trumpets,
  The Black Holes played the bass,
The Comets were the clarinets,
  The concert hall was Space.

The Stars were violins,
  The Angels sang in thirds,
The Planets danced a minuet,
  Jehovah wrote the words.

And still they sing together,
  And with the inner ears
The clear-souled man can listen yet:
  The music of the spheres.

Hymn: In the Dawning of Creation
Job 38:7

To the tune of "Jupiter's Theme,"
from Gustav Holst, *The Planets*

In the dawning of creation the stars together sang;
In harmonious equations their silver voices rang.
And the angels contemplated the beauty of the Lord
Seen in what He'd created and heard in every chord.
Still the symphony continues, its rich and lyric lines
Now resounding in the venues of human hearts and minds.

So we praise Thee, great Jehovah for all that thou hast made,
From the quarks to supernovas, before our minds displayed.
And You gave to us our senses, which find missives everywhere,
Breaking through our defenses with news that You are there.
Thus the firmament declareth through all its mighty frame
The clear message that it beareth: the glory of Thy name!

On What May Be Seen While Looking North from a Ridge-top in Athens, GA

Looking up (as I have often done),
    You see three ridges marching north from here,
    Unless the mist should melt them into one.
    But on rare days--say, eight or ten a year--
When some storm's maybe blown the air as clear
    As it can ever get, the sun goes down,
    And in it rays obliquely seems to peer
    Across the ridges' backs, as if it found
Some vision there worth staring at. The town
    Grows silent as the day draws to its close,
    And one lone walker looks up from the ground
    And stops dead still and stares--and stares--and knows
The sun's sight. Empty air before his eye
    Splits open, and the mountains fill the sky.

A String of Pearls

The light lit on the light leaves, lost
All its momentum there, and made
A curious transition, crossed
Into the softer light of shade.
The leaves, new light shed on them, glossed
With new significances, played
A game of wit and lightly tossed
Off puns and paradoxes, prayed
The wind to answer. She obeyed
And joined her most light-hearted voice:
Thus air-light leaves in serenade
May teach the spirit to rejoice.

The soul also rejoices when
The growling thunderstorm comes near
To scare away the heat that's been
Clogging up the atmosphere.
The subtle intensity within
That's not, but is akin to, fear
Is suddenly shattered by the din
That lets you know the thing is here.
With washing rain and lightning clear
The storm is sent; it has no choice
But to go on its wild career
And teach the spirit to rejoice.

Likewise the joyful mountain stream,
Hearing the voices of the leaves
And wind and rain and lightning, teams
Them all together; whence she weaves
One flowing tapestry which seems
A richer thing than man conceives
In sleep or in his waking dreams.
Beneath enchanted forest eaves
He hears it, and almost believes
It is a nymph's or naiad's voice.
It soothes, stings deep, enriches, grieves,
And makes the spirit to rejoice.

Rejoicing in the verbal skills
Displayed by her melodic strains,
The stream leaps lightly down the hills,
Spending all the speed she gains
In song and laughter as she spills
Herself toward the coastal plains.
Gradually then her song she stills:
A stately current which contains
The echoes of a thousand rains,
She bows before a greater voice,

Flows all into it, yet retains
Her own full spirit to rejoice.

Rejoicing in the gift, the sea
Receives her homage and returns
The voices to the air, and we
Hear once again the song that burns
In Nature's heart. Wild and free,
Our own blood answers it and yearns
To fly with the light wind and see
The water's path as it returns
To light on mountain leaves and ferns
And once more in the streams to voice
The song, where air-light-leaf-rain learns
To teach the spirit to rejoice.

Firmament

Thin clouds set by the moon aglow;
Concentric circles fade away:
White like sun on face of snow
Melts through silver into gray.
The surface is not smooth, but creased:
Rents and patches, not a few,
Hurried on from West to East,
Sometimes let a star shine through.
Frame it all with stands of pine,
Silent shapes against the light.
Shifting shadows redefine
Modulating moods of night.

Two Essays in Terza Rima

I

The swooping, darting, soar-song flock of birds
That swift across the sunset takes its flight
Says something that cannot be said by words.

The piercing of the stars through deepening night
Takes up the same theme, each in perfect time
And in a burning pitch to match its height.

The moon on wings of the same song doth climb
And wax and wane, and never miss a turn
To treat the clouds like words that poets rhyme.

And just before the dawn begins to burn
A hole in the dark tapestry of night
And light dew-jewels in cobweb, leaf, and fern,

A distant, glowing, cottage-window light
Speaks of shelter, breakfast, warmth, and peace,
A circle of love formed firm against the night

To join the birds, stars, moon, dawn in the east
And sing the self-same song. Oh, seek to grasp,
For seek to grasp we must, and never cease,

These will-o'-the-wisp, elusive notes that pass
Through restless minds like soft winds through the grass.

II

George Herbert tells us that You withheld Rest
From all the blessings that You gave to man
So that we might be tossed unto Your breast

And not be satisfied with aught less than
That supreme Good for which we all were made.
And, I confess, that seems to have been Your plan

In dealing with men like me, so apt to trade
The greater for the lesser good and lose
Both in the process, as we watch them fade.

For whether paths of planets I peruse,
Or watch the wandering of the autumn leaves,
Or see the sunset or sunrise's hues,

That age-old wandering impulse I receive:
To leave behind old earth's confining ring
And find the lasting Good we can't conceive.

It is not of themselves that the spheres sing,
But of the one who wrote their melody.
It is the Truth, the Life. It is the thing

Some hide from, some pursue, and some few see:
Our hearts are restless 'til they rest in Thee.

Proposed:
That the Modern Scientific World-View, In its Euphoria over Learning How to do Neat Things with Matter, Has Left Something out of the Equation

There was a time when men could see the sky,
    A grand cathedral vaulted and ablaze
    With myriad candles lifted up on high
    By nights for Vespers; in the brighter days,
The great Rose Window eastward shed its rays
    For Morning Prayer, and each and every flame
    Burned eloquent in litanies of praise,
    In fugues and canons to extol the Name.
But now the sky, though larger, is more tame,
    And modern man sees what he's taught to see:
    Vast numbers are just numbers all the same,
    Though multiplied toward infinity;
And quarks and quasars cannot speak to us
    Except as agitated forms of dust.

Except as agitated forms of dust,
    We don't know how to know the thing we are:
    The biochemistry of love is lust
    As an atomic furnace is a star,
And all that's known is particles at war.
    And yet we do know love, and yet we know
    That it and lust are infinitely far
    Apart. We know the stars and how they glow,
Though they know nothing of us here below.
    So even while we're slogging through the mire,
    We cannot help ourselves, but as we go
    We cock our heads to listen for the choir.
We know that half the truth is half a lie:
    There was a time when men could see the sky.

Sunrise: Adam Speaks

Distant, dim, the fortress mountains stood
    Beneath the fading light of a single star;
    And we looked out from the edges of the wood
    To watch the last light's funeral from afar,
Remembering how we first had seen the sun.
    We watched him rise in glory in the east,
    Rejoiced at seeing fear and darkness run
    To hide from his bright presence; but he ceased
To rise, and fell. We watched him slowly die
    In glory that could rival even his birth;
    Then saw his children in the darkened sky,
    Laughing! We could not understand their mirth
"Till, vaulting o'er the battlements, back he came
    And turned the leaden fog to golden flame.

Take off from LaGuardia
April, 1988

The contrast: nothing could be more alluring
    Than New York City shining in the last
    Light of evening; nothing less enduring,
    That vision off the wing-tip sliding past.
Her own lights are emerging like the slow
    Stars above, but eyes are mainly drawn
    To buildings like great tongues of flame that glow
    Awhile in gathering darkness, and are gone.
We all have strained for visions in the embers—
    They augur something, but who had the codes?
    The eyes enjoy the sight; the mind remembers,
    Below, the litter blowing in the roads.
The Light, then, and the Dark: but as we flew,
    The vision slipped away; the darkness grew.

Faith

It all depends upon your point of view:
    Up there above the clouds, the Sun is bright;
    Down here it seems the best that he can do
    Is heighten contrast, marking with his light
    The darker gray that makes the light gray white.
    They say the eye of Faith can see the blue
    Still there behind the sprawling gray, in spite
    Of surfaces that yield up not a clue:
Seeing the Truth depends upon your point of view.

Copernican Revolution

They say the earth goes spinning through the sky.
     The math is simpler if you view it thus,
     And doubtless it is so, but still to us
It is the sun that whirls and rushes by.
Yet we can see both visions if we try,
     Which raises one more issue to discuss:
     The simple question what you're going to trust,
What Reason says is true, or what the eye.

The eye informed by Reason is the best:
     The eastern rim drops dizzily away;
The roller coaster roars out of the west,
     Hurtles its riders on toward the day.
While most still lie oblivious in bed,
     The planetary plane tilts overhead.

New Every Morning

Scarlet fading into lavender,
     Backed with royal purple, rich and deep;
     The sharp horizon fades into a blur
     As imperceptibly as colors creep
Toward blackness lined with gray, while in the steep
     Vault above, the brightness of the moon
     And stars dissuades us yet awhile from sleep.
     Yes, this is how the sun declines from noon.
And now the stars ride overhead, but soon
     They too will fade. The cycle's never ceased:
     New variations on an ancient tune,
     Still new each morning. Slowly, in the East,
Rich reds and purples grow within the gray,
     A prelude to the glad reprise of Day.

Literary Motifs

Dusk to dusk and dawn to dawn,
Starlight, sunlight slip away.
Ubi Sunt, where have they gone?
All the sages cannot say.

Many things will be restored:
Sanctity in flesh of men;
But hours squandered from the hoard
Never will be seen again.

Ubi Sunt, where have they gone?
All the sages cannot say.
Hence the message of the dawn:
Carpe Diem! Seize the day.

ஒ Part III ଔ
Places and Critters

The Message

The standing tree was all
The meadow had to say.
It was not so very tall;
The wind could barely sway
It, pointing to the sky.
But you could hear it sigh
For something far away.
The standing tree was all
The meadow had to say.

Impression

Tree . . .
Wearing stars for rings on
Branching fingers,
Misty cloud for shawl,
We stand and grow
Together
For a moment.

On Watching Traffic on Illinois 294 from a Nearby Hill

Still searching, yet not knowing what
Lies at the end of our long quest,
We love our restless life, and yet
We sorely long for rest.

The First Thirty Minutes Out of Neel's Gap

It's amazing how the traffic noise can carry
        Across the ridges and the open spaces.
        This is the wilderness to eyes, but ears
Find it a good sight harder job to parry
        Civilization just by changing places;
        The legs pump, and a spray-paint blaze appears.

This is the Appalachian Trail! I say
        The sound of engines going through their paces
        Ought not to be a part of what one hears.
Just when you think you're far enough away,
        A trucker changes gears.

Inscape:
Or, the Idea of Order at Tallulah River

The swooping, soaring bat had no business to be
    Abroad so early, so fine a sun-filled day,
    But he was. He stirred our pulse as he skirted the tree
    And, falcon-like, stooped on his unseen insect prey.
Around that tree like a shuttle he wove his way,
    Now fluttering lightness of leaf, now diving weight;
    The field became a stage for a mystery play,
    A loom for the warp and woof of insect fate.
Yet more than the doom of bugs he caught and ate
    Was at stake in that circle of sun in the shadowy hills:
    Could the terrible grace of his course such a vortex create,
    A confluence of circling harmonies, forces, wills?
His flight stirred the air like a Word, a divine decree,
    And made the meadow a world with a still-point tree.

Shope Fork, NC: An Early Start

"Tonight the Fog will come to the bottoms to keep
    A tryst with his bride, the River. In the morning,
    If we are careful, we'll catch him quite asleep
    Right here on the bank beside her still, scorning
To notice the stars fading, to take warning,
    Knowing it takes 'most half a day for the sun
    To reach this valley floor with any warming.
    So over the meadow he spreads his blanket, spun
Of moonlight that shines on when the moon is done."
    The walkers were careful not to disturb the pair
    Of lovers as they left. When the peaks were won,
    They returned; the River alone was waiting there.
"Where does he go? No one has seen it aright.
    I only know he'll be back again tonight."

Dayhiker's Dilemma

Free from the load of tent and sleeping bag,
    You pay by being more a slave to Time.
    Measure it by watch or sun, the snag
    Is there, though slopes are easier to climb.
It is the time you have to turn around
    To make it back to camp or car by night.
    It is a law inexorable, profound,
    And it will win (though not without a fight!).
It's best to set a time that has some play;
    You cannot go but what you feel the spell.
    The hidden barrier that bars your way
    Asks to be pushed a bit, e'er it can quell
The voice that calls you on. It has no end:
    The lure of what lies just around the bend.

Eccentric

The buzzards circled silently,
Hardly needing to move their wings at all.
There were four of them,
And I stood stone still in their midst.
They were intent on something,
And their circle narrowed;
And I stood stone still,
Hardly daring to breathe
As their many-fingered wings floated motionless,
Not even twenty feet from my face.
And the circle narrowed,
And I stood stone still.
And I was glad
To have beheld their gaunt, ungainly grace
As their circle narrowed
And I stood stone still;
And I rejoiced
To find myself alive and still
Somewhat removed from their center.
And I remembered
How the ancient theologians defined God as a circle
Whose center was everywhere and whose circumference
Was nowhere.
And I understood
That if a man can find his center there,
He need not then concern himself thereafter
With his relationship to any other circle.
And their circle narrowed,
And I stood . . .
Stone . . .
Still.

Time at the Seaside:
The Shell in the Hand, Jekyll Island, 1984

The beach curves away forever, winding
    Its arms around the rear horizon, vast
    In reach as is the ocean flowing past.
The waves curve and break, forever finding
The sand, and in their surging ever grinding
    To smoothness shell and hull and sunken mast
    Until they wear to nothingness at last,
While still the waves roll on--the law is binding.

And I have seen the shell upon the shore
    Too often swept away by waves and slammed
    Back sandward past all smoothing, 'til it crumbles
To dust and dullness, is a shell no more.
    It's more than just the vastness here that humbles:
    It's this bright hardness to the same fate damned.

A Metaphor Glimpsed

The dog shifted in its sleep and sighed,
As the fire shifted and popped in its downward slide
To entropy and ashes. The man awoke
Just long enough to see, through sparks and smoke,
Successive layers of leaves and burning stars.
He thought of lightning bugs in Mason Jars,
Captured (to be set free again, not to keep)
In years long past, and then went back to sleep,
Wondering if sparks were starlight that the wood
Had caught and now set free again for good.
The leaves were whispering--were they saying "Yes?"
The smoke knew, but, reluctant to confess,
Maintained its silence and left the man to guess.

A Flicker of Hope

The world was thick, grey fog and shiny, black
Uplifted limbs of trees, and falling rain,
And mud, and water running in the track
And dripping from the twigs. My window pane
Could scarcely shut it out; into my brain
It came without resistance, wet and cold,
And drumming endlessly its dull refrain
Of all things growing, slowly growing old.
For weeks, thus. Once more into bed I rolled,
And woke to find the rain had turned to dew,
And all the dew the sun had turned to gold.
Colaptes Auratus, the Common Flicker, flew
Into my garden. Nothing was less true
About him than the "common" in his name.
A more uncommon creature never drew
The sun's rays with such concentrated aim
To fan his chevroned shoulders into flame:
Sharp red amidst the gold upon the brown-
Piled rug of pine straw into which he came
To look for bugs to eat. I hope he found
Some juicy ones; I know that he brought down
With him the wind that drove the clouds away
And scattered all that gold upon the ground.
And I would give much more than bugs for pay,
After such a damp and dark dismay,
To see again the long-lost light of day.

Conversation with a Backpacker

There is a path that slowly winds its way
Into the Hills. In sudden switchbacks up
It rises from the Tallulah River basin
In North Car'lina, and curls around along
The ridges until it crosses the bowl between
Big Scaly and Standing Indian; then, back down
It curves to join the Tallulah once again
In northern Georgia where the valley's broader.
It was a road put in to bring logs out,
But that was many years ago. Today
It seldom sees a truck, though I have met
The hoofprints of a burro coming down,
Plain where the ground was soft from last week's rain
Or in white scars where the iron had struck the sparks
Out of the flinty rocks in steeper places.
The beeches have grown for thirty years back in,
Along with scattered stands of birch and hemlock,
And hulks of patriarchs the woodsmen left
As monuments to the forest's former glory,
And the ever-present patches of rhododendron.
Except for the week-old marks of man-shod hooves
And the absence of older trees in the mist of the roadway,
There was little sign that men had come that way
Since the fathers of the beeches had been laid low.
Were it not for the shelter by the spring
With names and dates inscribed in candle-smoke
Upon the beams as a memorial,
You might have thought that place had been forgotten.

Between the peaks the land is almost flat
And opens in what you'd almost call a meadow,
And there the spring comes up beside the shelter
And almost forms a pond before it forms

The stream which forms Beech Creek, which almost gets
To be a river itself before the Tallulah
Deprives it of its name on down the valley.
There where the water is gentle the deer come
To drink and browse in the quiet of the morning
Before the sun can look in over the broad
Shoulder of Standing Indian, who stands guard
Above them there. If you are there some morning
You might see elven maidens in the distance,
Appearing and disappearing between the tree trunks.
Look closer and they will resolve themselves
Into the deer's white rumps as they go bounding
Across the ground. And now has come the time
You must be very still and very quiet.
You'll want the camera from your pack, of course,
But if you move to get it, however slowly,
The rumps will flash just once more and be gone.
Resist temptation. Clutch your bowl of oatmeal
And feel the heat go slowly out of it
As it goes still more slowly out of the fire
And up with the smoke in a grey, spiraled column
That could be one of the trunks of the young birches
'Round which the doe steps out into the clearing,
No more than twenty feet from where you sit.
She looks at you, and you are sure she sees you.
She stands and stares as motionless as you do.
Then, being satisfied you're not a hunter
(It's said they know the day the season opens,
And what guns are, and partly I believe it),
The graceful head goes down and starts to tear
Away the undergrowth. No, "tear" is wrong--
For later when you go there, you will find
The leaves and stems are clipped away as neatly
As you could do it with a pair of hedge-shears.
But now, this living thing that stands before you,
Its breath as white as yours in the cold air!

Up here she wanders and lives out her life
Within the ancient hills and infant forest,
Depending on no man to come and feed her.
She mates and bears her young and crops her leaves
And dances with her fellows in the forest
And warily sniffs the air for signs of hunters
(As she does now: see how the head comes up
With eyes and ears and nose all sharply pointed
Toward me at the slightest sound or movement
For a brief eternity of fierce attention
To see if I am still behaving myself.
Then, satisfied, the slender neck goes down
To feed again). All this she does and more,
And would even if I'd never come to see her.

You've seen deer in the zoos, no doubt, so tame
That children feed them milk from baby bottles,
And beautiful they are, but not the same.
The camera could not have told the difference
If I had gotten to it. Paint on canvas,
Fanciful words on paper about elf-maidens,
Suggest it merely. You must go yourself
And catch you own glimpse of the mystery.
There is no guarantee that you'll see anything,
But give up guarantees, and go. Remember,
Grace comes to whom it will. There's no explaining
Just why it touches one and not another.
You must be very still and very quiet.
Then if the deer comes, take it as a gift
Unearned. You are her uninvited guest;
You are a pilgrim and a stranger here:
The spring and meadow high between the mountains
Belong to her and to her kind forever.

Lament

The mole was dead upon the ground;
He did not move when he was poked.
His coat was sleek, his body round,
     His life revoked.

His parts seemed not to coincide:
His hands were stuck on at the wrist;
He was long-nosed and squinty-eyed,
     A humorist.

He looked too healthy to be dead;
His feet were white, his face was droll,
But he was tragic dust instead
     Of comic mole.

Mountain Memory

The mountains do not sleep when the sun goes down.
I have been nose to nose with a spotted skunk
Who came to eat the granola I had spilled
At supper, and then decided to find out
What kind of creature was a sleeping bag,
And ask it why it slept when all the other
More sensible creatures were up foraging,
And what was it doing in his backyard, anyway?
He learned to his surprise it was a skin
For an even stranger creature called a man.
(Just what he would have thought had he found out
It was detachable, I dared not ask him.)
What shined more brightly, his eyes or his sleek coat?
I mustn't frighten him, but ought I let
Him stay this close? And what choice did I have?
In his own way, no doubt, he asked himself
Much the same questions about me, though likely
He was less impressed than I was by the awesome
Beauty of the creature he had met,
And less torn between joy and apprehension,
And much more sure of just what he would do
If the other varmint should look too aggressive.
For a time we stared and asked our silent questions,
Then some noise startled him and he was gone.
It seemed that we had made a goodly trade:
A few crumbs of granola for a night
Of wonder and delight, and each of us
Was sure he had the best end of the bargain.

May 6, 1972

There is naught like a lake, hill-nestled, sky-nurtured,
And the arrow-smooth skimming of sleek prophet birds
And the wind-voice that speaks from wet water-weeds writhing
To remind one that man's favorite figures of atoms
Explain precisely nothing.

Pinchincha

I have walked and talked intimately with the clouds
On the slopes of Pinchincha,
And I have left the clouds behind and gone
Where they did not care to follow.
And there I stood alone with the universe and sang
Songs of praise to its Creator.
And there I learned wisdom that cannot be made into poems,
But this I can tell you:
It is difficult to doubt Him when He thunders at you
With such silence.

Messiah College Campus, June 1983

Imagine the place:
Rolling hills of southern Pennsylvania,
Yellow Breeches Creek cutting through them.
It must have earned its name a ways upstream,
For here it is a river in its own right,
A hundred feet across, three deep,
With just a hint of mountain songs it sings
No doubt as a creek that's worthy of the name.
Soon it will flow into the Juniata.
Here it makes its way beneath the footbridge
That swings across it and the covered bridge
For cars that is just visible upstream.
It's early evening, maybe half past nine.
The muted voices of stream and leaf serve only
To accentuate the silence. Even the creaking
Footbridge cables hardly can do more
Than that. The moon stands directly over
The covered bridge, trees with lifted branches
Framing a lane to the sky. In the distance,
Not visible itself beyond the car-bridge,
A campfire sends its flames lightly skipping
Toward you down the water like small stones
That do not sink: paths of gold on the water,
The moon doing the same thing in silver.
The stars are hidden in the lingering summer
Haze; lightning bugs take their places.
The eyes find more light in the growing darkness,
Shining from more metals in the water:
Dark iron lies along the sides,
Lurking in the shadows of the trees;
In the center, open to the sky,
Mercury--these deep, the gold and silver
Upon the surface, light that's born on waves,

Pulling apart, moving under your feet,
Always coming on but never arriving,
Always breaking up but never quite
Destroyed or lost. A screech-owl's rasping brings
The taste of metal up into your mouth
And cancels instantly the muggy heat.
This is cold steel! It tears the air again,
Then through that opening pours the breeze that speaks
Of thunderstorms. The lightning tears the air,
Reminding you Time has not truly stopped
(Though you would swear it paused, if only briefly),
And you remember you are wanted elsewhere,
And you remember that this too is gold.

The Rockies at Night
(From Fort Collins)

The sky was dark, the mountain darker still;
　　　Electric lights climbed halfway up the side,
　　　Then Nothingness, and then a jagged line
Where stars began. It was enough to chill
　　　The bones, to make you want to run and hide,
　　　That yawning gap where light refused to shine.

Stubborn memories fetched back from day,
　　　Clung to for the permanence implied
　　　Of solid rock and Ponderosa Pine,
Keep us from the abyss--yet, still I say,
　　　It was a sign.

Continental Divide

Only a matter of minutes ago
       The water in this stream
Was part of a bank of solid snow.
Now it splashes down to the rocks below,
Then on to the Gulf of Mexico.
       It certainly doesn't seem
As if, a hundred yards or less
Away, o'er an imperceptible crest,
Another stream should be heading West
       In search of a different sea.
Two windblown snowflakes came to rest
An inch apart. Who could have guessed
That such a widely divergent quest
       Should be their destiny?
But if you've watched the snowflakes blow
And felt how strongly rivers flow
And seen how men and women grow
By making choices that seem so
Insignificant—then you know
       That such a thing can be.

The Rockies and Snow Wolf Lodge
A Glimpse

Times when all is still
And not an aspen leaf is stirring;
Times the wind is shrill
And air and leaf and hair are churning;
Sunlight on the hill
Turns leaves to tongues of fire burning;
A bracing Autumn chill
Strangely sets the heart to yearning.

Up from Snow Wolf
"Business" in the Rockies

The lodge in its protected vale is higher
Than anything the Smokies have to offer.
The old dirt road climbs steadily up from there
For two, three miles. The pines and quaking aspens
Give way to spruce and fir. A golden eagle
Sails effortlessly past. It's hunting season,
So tracks are all you'll see of elk or deer.
A magpie or a Colorado jay
Might squawk at you suspiciously, then turn
Aside to go about his birdly business.
What is your business? Just to soak it in.
You smile at that and take another step,
Sighing at how few of them remain
Before you have to turn yourself around
With time enough to reach the lodge again
In time for supper and ahead of sunset.
So savor that step, and the next one too.
All told, it's been a banner day for business.

Joyce Kilmer Memorial Forest

Eyes meandering across
The tangled rootwork will discern
A rich ubiquity of moss,
A lush fecundity of fern.

The trunks, like Grecian columns, soar
Toward a roof of leaves so high
Above you on the forest floor,
It seems they must support the sky.

Between the columns, standing there
As if suspended in a dream,
No sound disturbs the scented air
Except the murmur of a stream.

You listen with expectant ear
For what the brooding silence hints.
You are a passing stranger here,
Fit place for one of Tolkien's Ents.

Jogging, Sunrise, Milford Church Road and Austell Road
Mach 28, 1984

Dog, possum; near, far:
What swift destiny or star
Left the two of you where you are?
Dog, possum; kin, strange:
Night, road, car--change.
Soon bereft of all your range.

Collie: silky, golden tress,
Hand invited to caress
Vision still of loveliness;
Face full of loyal trust.
Possum: tattered, ratty dress,
Alien eyes, expressionless;
Both now only empty crust.
Seasons come and seasons go.
Though the process will be slow
(Scaling, flake by flake, of rust),
Rain, sun, the status quo:
Both in winds of Fall will blow
Indiscriminately dust.

Possum, dog; strange kin:
Could such a small break in the skin
Let the creeping chaos in?
Possum, dog; far, near:
Fate was quirky, fortune queer
To toss you two together here.

Apocalypse

It was a bare place, despite the vegetation.
There was grass on the rounded hills, the long slopes,
A few trees standing, just enough
To make you notice that there were not more.
They were dark evergreens, stooped with age.
They did not stand in bunches, but alone,
Spread out like silent sentinels to watch
The years and keep a record of their doings.
There was wind in the grass and the twisted limbs.
        There was
Too little between a man and the horizon.
You ought to have to climb awhile before
The sky can open up and leave you standing
Emptied out of everything but wonder.
You ought to have to go past dripping ferns,
Cool with water seeping from the rocks.
The graceful arms of trees should pull back slowly
To open in an unexpected meadow,
Then fold together again to receive you back.
It ought to be a thing you have to seek,
Perhaps unconsciously, and then return from
Weakened and yet stronger for the journey.
It is not always so, for there was grass
On rounded hills, and wind was in the grass,
And the sky was all around you, all around you,
And lonely trees told tales that had no words.

Farewell to Snoopie

The once lithe body lay too large, too long.
The proportions were off, the head's angle strange:
Something about it certainly was wrong.

Something about the way the limp legs hung
Boded less wandering, a shrunken range.
The once lithe body lay too large, too long.

Never before had I seen her without a song
Of bugle-haunted greetings in glad refrains.
Something about it certainly was wrong.

The silk ears, once in gay abandon flung,
Were still, and their position did not change:
The once lithe body lay too large, too long.

A fly crawled slowly undisturbed along
The nose. Fur rose in winds foreboding rains.
Something about it certainly was wrong.

And standing there, I felt no longer young,
And thought age no great bargain in exchange.
The once lithe body lay too large, too long;
Something about it certainly was wrong.

Nativity

It pushes up from down below;
The hillside slopes and drops away:
And so the stream begins to flow —
Exactly where, I cannot say.

Where leaves have fallen, there they lie;
The rain soaks through them day by day.
Slowly the top layers dry —
Exactly when, I cannot say.

And then the leaves are wet again:
The damp spreads downhill like a ray.
It gathers to a trickle then —
Exactly how, I cannot say.

Imperceptibly its force
Collects, 'til in a bed of clay
(The leaves expelled) it makes its course —
Exactly where, I cannot say.

Although the stream is very young,
It has some things it wants to say:
You realize it's found its tongue —
Exactly when, I cannot say.

It disappears beneath a stone;
Then suddenly, several yards away,
It's back again — and t has grown.
Exactly how, I cannot say.

It pushes up from down below;
The hillside slopes and drops away;
And so the stream begins to flow —
Exactly where, I cannot say.

Quail

Flash! flushed, it rushes and flurrying flies,
    No covey, but one lone quail, across the grass;
    While fluttering like its flight, the notes it cries
    Float flute-trilled thrills, through back the hushed air
        pass.
Oh fleet flinger of wing-beats into space,
    Oh sweet singer to carol the quickening dawn,
    One breathless, trembling moment saw you race
    The sun to the distant trees, and you were gone.
Hopkins held all Nature was news of God:
    Free windhover, caged lark, unleaving grove,
    Stippled trout, generations that trod and trod--
    And I'd thought, "What treasure if true then, Nature's
        trove!"
And standing there, startled and shaken by your shimmering
    flight,
    I knew beyond all doubt that he was right.

Accuracy

It is not blue, no matter what they say.
    The basic livery, though trimmed in white,
    Is equal parts of brown and green and gray.
You might believe it of a winter's day,
    But even in the warmest summer light,
    It is not blue, no matter what they say.
Shades of blue? The Mediterranean may;
    The cold Atlantic offers us a sight
    Of equal parts of brown and green and gray.
A hunting pelican plunges in the spray;
    The seagull soars and calls out in his flight,
    "It is not blue, not matter what they say."
Near the breakers, laughing children play,
    Erecting castles walled against the might
    Of equal parts of brown and green and gray.
The Poet too pursues it his own way—
    To see and think and try to get it right:
    It is not blue, no matter what they say,
But equal parts of brown and green and gray.

Thoughts from St. Simons

The peace of Christchurch, the old oak
Beneath whose branches Wesley spoke;
The Spanish Moss, like wisps of smoke.

Here once flew the Union Jack;
The Redcoats kept the Spaniard back.
Now glass protects the artifact.

Beneath the sun, Frederica Town:
The tabby walls have all come down—
Foundations gaping in the ground.

The walls are tall, without a breach
In children's castles on the beach,
But all within the high tide's reach.

The sound of surf, the seagull's cry,
The crab that passes sideways by,
An endless question asking why.

The tracks the grass makes in the sand,
A seashell nestled in the hand,
The endless quest to understand.

The circling sea, gray-green in hue,
White sails against a sky of blue;
The Good, the Beautiful, the True.

Black Mountain Road and Highway 17 North Habersham County, GA

Over eighty species he had counted
    Of plants and animals within a mile.
    He knew that figure probably amounted
    To just a tenth of what one could compile
Who really knew his stuff. Still, he could smile
    At all the fertile superfluity
    That seemed to constitute the Maker's style.
    Yet all this infinite diversity
Was structured in a vast congruity
    You could in reason call a universe.
    Black-eyed Susans, several brands of bee,
    Five kinds of oak, three pines, magnolias, firs,
Eastern bluebird, wood-dove, cardinal, crow:
    The pure, white beam is scattered thus below.

Newfound Gap, March 2004

The upward slopes were potent to entice
    The feet; the snow-clad fir and swirling cloud,
    The eye. The weather had suppressed the crowd.
It seemed a perfect chance. So, in a trice
I left. The bitter cold soon felt quite nice
    As I toiled upward. For a while I plowed
    Ahead, but soon my trek was disallowed
By snow that passing feet had turned to ice.

To climb was fine. "But what about descending?
    In hiking, what goes up must come back down,"
    The Brain observed, and so the trip was over.
It seemed a great defeat, that journey's ending.
    The Brain had won. But, though it came around,
    The Heart sighed, yearning still to be a rover.

Parallel

The river seems to wander aimlessly,
But in the end it always finds the sea.
The Sun dips West beyond the sight of men,
But in the East brings back its light again.
A little leaven hidden in the dough
Will lose itself, but so the loaf will grow.
The corn that goes into the earth to die
Will in the Spring mount up toward the sky.
Although the stream meanders in its course,
Upstream infallibly you'll find its source.
Thus doubly God His wisdom will disclose:
Speaks in the Word what in the world He shows.

ဢ Part IV ଔ
Times and Faces

Carpentry

Sweet to the nose but rough to the hands, the pine
Boards must be sawed just so and stacked in line,
Not resting, lest they warp, upon the ground,
Until their turn has come to be nailed down
With all their fellows, framing floor or wall.
Here will be the kitchen, there the hall,
And there a bedroom with its bath, and there
A porch on which to breathe the summer air,
All laced with starlight when the night is warm,
And wonder if the distant thunderstorm
Or one of its wild kin will come and pay
A boisterous visit e're the break of day.
But that is weeks off, yet. For now, the wide-
Spaced workmen must be all kept well supplied
With lumber hauled up from the pre-sawed stack
By means of someone's hands and someone's back.
When palms grow tender, fingers stiff, back sore,
The job has just begun; you carry more.
And so the summer passed. I often stopped
At close of day when the last load was dropped
And thought, "In this I'm not alone: my Lord's
Hands also were worn raw by rough pine boards."

The Walk

"You're sure you know the way back to the car?"

"Of course. We simply have to go downhill
Until we hit the river, then turn right,
And follow it upstream. It can't be far."

"It better not be."
                    "Well, it isn't. Still,
The sun is setting quickly--not that night
Would be unpleasant if it caught us here.
The air's--but wait a minute--here we are!"

The river suddenly shimmered in the light
Of half a red sun and one pure white star.
The girl released her small, half pleasant fear,
And dropped it in the stream without a sound;
It just as silently floated out of sight.

"See, there's the path back to the road, as clear
As day." His whispered words were almost drowned
Out by a cricket and a timid wave
That flirted with the shore and with the ear.

"I wish I'd known before that you were bound
To cut cross-country, so I could have saved
These silly shoes from all the scuffs and mud
And worn my walking boots."
                            He looked around
And saw her teasing smile. "You see, the paved
Roads couldn't satisfy my roving blood.
I didn't foresee, either, that the ground
Untrod beneath those trees would have the pull
It did. My feet were helpless to resist

The call."
  She laughed, "And have you ever found
It otherwise?"
                              "I hope I never do.
Why, think of all the things we would have missed."

"Like blisters, scratches, aching feet . . ."
                              "And you
And me alone with leaves, and clouds, and sun,
And evening flowing, like the river, slow . . ."

She took his hand, and sighed, and said, "I know."

The Poet to His Daughter at Eighteen Months

What a mystery, my little friend,
You are, what an enigma to me now!
Not all your forty words can tell me how
The least thing in this world appears to you.
And yet, the snatches that I apprehend:
A magic landscape now springs into view,
Now fades into the mist, and springs anew,
But leaves not one clear image in the end.
Oh, there will come a day when you can grope
About for metaphors that can let me
See through your eyes, and find them too, I hope.
But then, alas! the vision will not be
This bright one that I long so now to see.

The North Georgia Mountains
and Kate Merritt Maxwell

You can feel them rising underneath the ground
Before you see them rising in the air.
I think it is because they're gathering strength
For the great push that brings them into view,
Their bent backs all hunched up against the sky.
The earth has backbones there, and when you stand
Upon it you can feel them. Just don't ask
What sense reveals it, for there is no answer
Except the changing rhythms of the blood.

I think the blood must somehow feel the call
Of all the springs that rise up with the mountains
Just to spill themselves in endless laughter
Helter-skelter down the rocky stream beds
So water, wind, and stone can sing together
To an attentive audience of pine trees.
We are allowed to overhear the music:
It always seems to be reminding us
Of something in ourselves we have no name for
And easily forget down in the flatlands.
I will not say the voices in the streams
Are singing to us, but we overhear them
And dare not say they do not sing to Someone.
And though we are not Someone, we are someone,
Which may be why we are allowed to listen
And, in not understanding, understand.

I knew a lady in Cornelia, who
Is buried within sight of where the mountains
First poke their faces over the horizon.
For when I traveled north to preach the funeral,
I didn't know the mountains could be seen there;
But in the church as I stood by the coffin
And saw the silent men and weeping women
And spoke of Sin and Death and Resurrection,
From far away I felt their roots beneath me,
Which somehow gave me strength to carry on;
Then later, at the burial site, I saw them.

That day I did not drive on to the mountains,
Though I have visited them often since
And someday will go there and not return.
When that day comes, I'm sure that I will meet her,
And when I do I think she will be singing.
I will sing the wind, and she the water,
And there will be Someone to sing the rock
(Of ages, cleft for me, will be the tune).
In that singing will the Song be clearer
Than we had ever heard it here before,
And we will surely understand it better,
And in that understanding, understand.

Kilgo

We never did get to the woods together.
We'd meet up in his air-conditioned office
From time to time to swap a tale or two.
He'd find a chair beneath a pile of papers
For me, beneath a pile of books for him,
And we'd lament the state of education
And then get on to more important things:
How quiet dawn is in a river swamp,
How sharp the wind blows over Albert's Mountain,
The steam a plate of grits makes on a table
When frost is on the sedge outside the window,
The best last lines in all of literature
(They must be Isaac Walton's *Life of Donne*
And then "The Life and Death of Cousin Lucius").
We'd quote from C.S. Lewis, Tolkien, Faulkner,
Or Robert Frost, or Flannery O'Connor;
We loved the words that named the things we loved.
We even tried some naming of our own--
He'd read his stories, and I'd read my poems,
Testing lines like newly mounted axe-heads
For balance and a clean and compact stroke:
The different rhythm life has on the trail--
I said, "Three days away from clocks you feel it";
The trout he caught high in a mountain stream
In pools between the rapids and the falls--
"No gift comes cleaner from the hand of God."
His book was *Deep Enough for Ivorybills*.
He meant woodpeckers in a cypress swamp;
I take it and apply it to his soul.
We love the words that name the things we love,
And one among the cleaner strokes is "Jim."

For Flannery

The body was alive. The evidence
Is that her fingers, for pure nervousness,
Caressed the chair's arm, and that was enough;
The rest was calm, the eyes demure. The voice
Was slow and hesitant, but when it had
A chance to build momentum it could carry
The burden of a thought or two, and drive them
Directly, if gently, toward the heart of things.
(The eyes would then look up, as if to follow
The words and make sure they were going straight.)
The body was alive, there is no doubt.
A fifteen-minute strip of celluloid
Is proof, and there are other witnesses
Whose bodies are still living, and will be,
I reckon, for another couple decades.
The body is cold dust and brittle bone,
And blind as Hazel Motes. But take the cold,
Thin strip of plastic, add electric light,
A motor, and some other gadgetry,
It will be warm and soft again, or seem so.

We most of us belong to Hazel's church:
Our lame don't walk, our blind don't see, our dead
Stay put, our Jesus has no blood to spare,
Despite what we recite on Sunday mornings.
The body stalks from tree to tree behind us.
Its hands fidget in embarrassment;
Its eyes occasionally look up. (Be sure
That's only in the mind. The body still
Lies quiet--even now the bones are crumbling.)
Be sure you do not look into the eyes.
If once you do, you are forever lost,

Your well-adjusted modern life in shambles;
Jesus, striding through the point of light
Behind the pupils, will lay hold of you.
"The prophet that I raise up from her words
Will burn your eyes clean!" There will be no way
To keep out even resurrections, then,
Or Jesus' blood. And you will see the body
Living, and it will not be on film.

Too Many Birthdays

"What seems to be the trouble, Mr. Williams?" – Physician
"Too many birthdays." – Thomas J. Williams, age 91

The leg-kick that gave leverage to pull
    The prop and get the old Lycoming started;
    The torque that wrist could put upon a wrench;
A head bent over his Bible and a full
    Support for ministers that were true-hearted;
    Integrity that wouldn't give an inch.

That is the way we all remember him
    Until "too many birthdays" came and thwarted
    The spirit in the body it still clinched
With wilted memory and withered limbs
    That made us want to flinch.

On My Grandmother's Father, His Wife, Minne Ellabella Huitt, and a Tenuous Connection with Robert E. Lee

William Forney Lee had a long, white, drooping mustache
And a black string tie in the pictures in the drawer
At my grandmother's house. She was all I knew of him,
The old photographs and the stories that she told:
How his father had been sick and couldn't go to fight the
     Yankees,
And old Marse Robert had come down himself to see him
And give such comfort as could be for such a woe,
And left him a daguerreotype, a new-fangled picture
Of himself on Traveler, and written on the bottom
With his own hand, "To my favorite nephew." That was all.
That was all! It was enough. To have such a contact
Was more than I have even yet begun to comprehend.
But was the story true? There wasn't any need to doubt it.
Her very own eyes had seen the picture more than once,
And that was back when she could see as well as anyone.
Well, now she is as old, almost, as William Forney's wife
Had been when I, a boy, barely able to remember,
Had been led up to the wheelchair where the tiny woman sat,
Her hair up in a bun, the whitest white I'd ever seen,
And someone shouted, "This is Vera Lee's boy, your great
     grandson,"
And slowly her ancient hand had reached out to touch me.
There was an old country house with a long porch, and horses
At the far end of the pasture, and a calf in the barn,
And bird-dogs in a pen who jumped up to lick my fingers.
There were long tables spread in the yard beneath the oak tree.
The spiced tea was strange on my tongue--I wouldn't drink it,
But there was chicken and dumplings and a giant birthday
     cake,
And water that you drank with a ladle from a bucket

That you cranked up creaking on a rope from the well.
It was all Great Grandma Lee, it was all the Birthday Dinner,
And it happened every year. When we came back again,
The horses and the bird-dogs were still there, but she was not.
Well, William Forney Lee had mouldered twenty years already,
And now twenty more have passed. The horses and the dogs
Have followed both their mistress and their master into dust.
The old house is gone; there is a new brick one now,
With all the modern plumbing, but it does not have a porch.
Only the old oak tree remains as a reminder,
And the pictures in the drawer, and the pictures in my mind.
"But where is the daguerrotype?" I ask, but get no answer.
"Oh surely it is somewhere in the family, but I can't say
Exactly where. It's been so long, there are so many branches."
As many as the branches of the oak that was a sapling
When William Forney's father took an unexpected present
From the kindest hand that ever held a sword. And I have
    touched
The wife of the son of the man who was that nephew of Marse
    Robert,
And oh, I wish that I had known, I wish that I had known!

Commentary, I Corinthians 15:17-19

It was two years ago the lightning struck
The oak tree in Great Grandma Lee's front yard
Whose branches were like tree trunks in their own right.
It seemed a fitting time to learn of it:
Great Grandma's daughter could not even leave
The car and hobble over to the gravesite
The day we buried Pa'pa Jones. They rolled
The window down so she could hear the service
Shouted over wind that made the young
And sturdy shake. It took two men to help her
From the car to the house. What little aid
Her limp legs gave was more than they could notice.
They finally got her propped up in a chair
Where she sat passive, still herself as death
Amidst the flux of relatives and friends
Bringing their pies and cakes and plates of chicken,
Conserving strength until someone should speak.
"Miss Grace, your husband was my Daddy's boss
At Silvercraft." She came alive and smiled:
"After he retired he tried to get
Bossy with me at home, and so I said,
'You want someone to boss, go back to work!'"
She could not keep it up, and soon retired
Back deep inside the skull, where, lithe and supple,
Her mind still lived and listened, thought, and waited
For the next voice to separate itself
Out from the general buzz. Meanwhile the crowd
Spilled out into the yard and hunched their backs
Up in their overcoats against the cold,
Noting how bare the place looked since the maples
Had lost their crowns to let the power lines
Get past unhindered. So then Cousin Baron,
Up from the old home-place in the country,

Spoke with pride and sadness of the Tree
Whose limbs had shaded Grace when hers were graceful:
"It was the oldest tree in Lincoln County.
We know Aunt Laney had a swing in it
When she was just a little girl, and if
She were alive she'd be a hundred-ninety.
It took the men two weeks to take it down.
The stump was nineteen feet across the base,
But hollow and rotten. When the lightning struck
We had no choice."
                              "That hurts," somebody said.
They seemed appropriate words for such a day,
Black and desolate in the dead of winter.
They say Time soothes old wounds, but do not mention
That it inflicts as many as it heals.
The wind blew 'til another season came.

               The world stood on the verge of Spring:
               The lightest mist or haze of green
               O'er lines of limbs was glimmering
               To blur the starker structures seen
               For half the year, now glistening
               With white of snow and sun, now dark
               Against the sky, enveloping
               With folded arms the moon or spark
               Of blazing star. So, lingering,
               They wait another week's increase
               Of leaves, whose subtle softening
               Of sight and sound will sigh, "Release
               Your vigilance against the cold!"
               And yet beneath their whispering
               I sense the limbs remembering
               The fate of every former Spring,
                         And feel them growing old.

We must await a stronger Spring than this.

All That's Left

Twelve years he had rested in the ground,
    His room, save for his absence, still unchanged.
    It could not last. The wheel of Time turns 'round.
    It does not matter how you have arranged
Your world; old Father Time will have his way.
    The day came then at last for Mom to leave.
    Assisted Living, where she now must stay,
    Had no room for Dad's stuff. With no reprieve,
It must be broken up. The siblings came
    For triage: trash, Good Will, what we could keep.
    Shotgun; altimeter; a model plane;
    Some photographs that make you want to weep:
"So 'til the Judgment, that yourself arise . . ."
    God grant the Bard's words be the truth, not lies!

๛ Part V ๙
Toccoa Falls: An Ode

It never ceases.
I sit here, barely out of sight and sound
Of all that water crashing to the ground,
And still the looming ledge of rock releases
    Into the air
A solid stream of liquid, curving down
And breaking up into a million pieces,
Each one a globe of pearl or diamond rare
To catch the sun or moonlight shining there:
A cataract of riches to astound
A Midas or a Solomon, all drowned
(Or better, reinvested) in the stream
Of wealth which blesses all the land around.
    Such is my theme:
Toccoa, "Beautiful" in Cherokee;
In any language--in reality--
A partial but an accurate exegesis.
    Oh Spirit of the River,
    Teach me to be a giver
As thou hast been, and help me to expound
In measured lines melodious and strong
Faithfully the meaning of the song
You sing, as playful as it is profound,
And having always as it rolls along
    One constant thesis:
Your Maker's face with grace and glory crowned.

It never ceases.
    Were I to go as far away
    As to the Indies or Cathay,
    And there remain a year or more
    Studying exotic lore,

Occupying thus my mind
With thoughts exalted and refined--
Were I to make an even longer stay,
Never seeing the red Georgia clay
Nor hearing your cascading water's roar
'Til I grew old and hoar--
And then at long last should I come back here
To feel again the coolness of your spray
And let your voice again refresh my ear
And watch again the way your waters fall,
Leaping headlong from the granite wall
(But leaving in return
In each inch of its crannies, nooks, and creases
A lush green tapestry of moss and fern),
I know that you would not have changed at all.

It never ceases.
It never ceases to amaze me how
When I've left gazing at you and my head
Lies weary and oblivious in my bed,
How even now,
Whether or not I'm standing by to stare
Or any creature even is aware,
Incessantly you pour
Your bounty forth and still have more to spare.
Where does it come from, this abundant store
Of living water leaping through the air?
The Heavens send the rains upon the hills,
And leaves on trees and on the forest floor
Will savor slowly every drop that spills
From Heaven's treasury;
That moisture, drop by tiny drop, distills
Through moss and soil and porous rock, until
It's filtered to a crystal purity.
And then in tiny rivulets and rills,
Trickling, joining, imperceptibly

It swells until it fills
A brook which joins a larger tributary,
Leaping over pebbles, light and airy,
Crescendoing until the tune it trills
                    Resounds across the hills
And valleys in a joyous symphony.
Thus, bubbling up in countless springs and fountains,
It forms the living bloodstream of the mountains,
An endless wellspring of vitality
Enveloping within its silver thread
The earth, the trees, the sky, the river bed--
The yearning of the water for the sea.
It is the cycle of the gift returned,
Accepted only to be freely given,
From sky to earth to sea and back to Heaven--
                    Not needing to be earned--
Open-handed, each in turn releases
The living water, flowing wild and free,
Embracing its eternal destiny--
                    It never ceases.

And how would someone write your history?
Before the White Man was the Cherokee;
Before the Red Man, none knows what eyes
May have gazed in wonder and surprise
                    Upon the mystery
Which shimmers in the hieroglyphs of spray
In patterns changing constantly, which play
Upon the wet, black rocks. Did they devise
Mythologies in an attempt to say
Back to you what you tried to say to them?
And in those tales, did anything come through,
                    However dim,
Which you would recognize as being true?
                    We do not know--
Nor how much further we would have to go

Until the hawk, the beaver, and the bear,
The silence of the forest standing there,
The mist that gathers in the morning air,
                    The rain, the snow,
The sunlight or the moonlight shining fair,
The hills above, the valley far below
Would be the only witnesses to see
Your waters flowing still in majesty.
                    We do not know--
Nor how much further we would have to go
To find the day you first began to flow,
What strange upheavals of the new-made earth
                    Brought you to birth.
Our earliest glimpses of your mysteries
Are in the legends of the Cherokees.

"When the Great Spirit came down to the land
To make the fathers of the sons of men,
He made the White Man from the ocean sand;
But then, not satisfied, he tried again,
And, scooping up the rich red Georgia clay
                    Into his hand,
He made a people with a ruddy skin
To wander where the laughing waters play.
We were the *Aniyunwiya*, the Principle Men,
Until the White Man took our land away.
Ku! That was a bitterness of heart
                    Beyond our greatest fears:
To tear the people and the land apart,
To see the old men stumbling by the carts
                    Upon the Trail of Tears;
Or Tsa-Li, haggard, hiding, holding out
Despite the soldiers scurrying about
Until the awful bargain reached his ears.
The terms were simple and the terms were plain:
For his blood spilled a remnant could remain.

And so the White Man made us 'civilized':
Broken, scattered, beaten, full of pain,
               Deceived, despised—
And we have never ever understood.
Sequoyah made us our own kind of letter,
               Marks that could
Talk Cherokee--and soon the White Man made
His holy Book in them. An old chief weighed
It carefully, and said, 'This Book is good.
I wonder that the White Man is not better,
Since he has had it for so very long.'
No, we have never ever understood.
               But long ago we knew
Unelanunhi, brighter than the sun,
Apportioner of light, and rain, and dew,
Who gives himself in water and in fire:
Descending in them from above he gives
His power to the earth, and life is born.
He comes down to the earth, and on it lives
The *yonah* and the *awi* swift to run,
               And from it grows the corn.
He gives himself in water and in fire,
And when we aspire
To give ourselves to him, it is the same;
               For we return
A portion of our crops in rising flame,
And when we make ourselves the offering
               We dance and sing
And go to water, where we try to give
Our spirits to the One who makes them live
And come out washed from grief and care and shame.
And though we could not know with certainty
               That we could please
The gods with ceremonies such as these,
It was the clearest vision we could see:
               As though there came

Just barely through the mist a single star
Whose light we, stumbling, followed from afar.
            The water and the flame:
They were the holy channels of exchange.
            And does it not seem strange
That we should grasp a clearer, surer Word--
            Does it not seem absurd
That from the liars and the cheats who took
Our land, we should receive the holy Book?
We never would have known God had a Son;
We never would have known what He has done.
And though some have believed (for God is good),
We still have never ever understood."

And probably will never understand.
But for a remnant on the reservation,
            The fruit of Tsa-Li slain,
Survivors of a free and mighty nation,
The Cherokee has vanished from the land.
But yet the lightning and the falling rain,
The river rushing toward the ocean sand,
The shining sun, the deer, the growing grain,
The seasons in their regular refrain--
The fire and the water--still remain.
And in those tales, did anything come through
 That you would recognize as being true?
Though we can never gather all the pieces
Or fit them in the puzzle to explain
All things, we are not left without a clue:
The fire and the water still remain.

            It never ceases.
Near the lonely mountain, Currahee,
A living image of eternity,
            Your endless flow
Saw the Red Man's nation come and go,

Saw the White Man's nation come and grow,
              And came to see
Another chapter in your history.
Is it something in the song you sing
That works unheard throughout the world to bring
Them all together in community
              Around your feet?
From every corner of the earth, they meet
Around you for a few short years, and then,
Subtly changed, they issue forth again
While others like them still are flooding in.
Young men and women, others not so young,
              With but one goal:
To learn the Message that can make life whole,
Transform the mind, regenerate the soul;
Engrave it on the heart, attune the tongue--
              And so be flung
Out to the farthest corners of the earth,
Bearing stories strange of death and birth,
Singing the Song that somehow must be sung.
              Could it have to do
With something in the tune they hear from you?
It started with one man who had a dream.
Dr. Richard Forrest was no fool.
He really didn't really have much of a scheme;
He surely had no money he could pool.
He figured, with the Bible as his creed,
And with his heavenly Father and His school,
The only thing he needed was a need.
The land north of Toccoa did look nice,
But twenty thousand dollars was the price.
"All I have is one ten-dollar bill."
              More than he could afford?
"I'll give you that right now to close the deal.
The Lord and I will be good for the rest."
The banker said, "Well, I can trust the Lord."

The crumpled bill was passed from hand to hand;
The preacher and the banker passed the test.
The Haddock Inn, a hundred acres, and
                    The waterfall:
Ten dollars and a prayer bought it all,
And so the school began.
And what was it that brought him to this place?
Was it some mysterious providence?
Or did he somehow sense a kind of sense
In the singing of your waters as they race?
We know that to Toccoa Falls they came,
                    And had not been here long
Living in the rhythms of your song,
Until the Haddock Inn went up in flame
And left the school in ashes smoldering.
But those intrepid scholars did not wince
Or falter in the song they'd come to sing:
                    They kept on studying.
Throughout the winter, on into the spring,
The college simply carried on in tents.
                    Were they insane?
Although the Inn that sheltered them was gone,
The fire and the water still remain:
The holy instruments of loss--and gain.
The college, stronger, simply carried on.

And the years passed like the waters as they flow,
And as they passed, they saw the campus grow.
The waters blessed the land as they flowed past
And flowed on 'til they reached the sea at last,
Where, mingling their song with the ocean's roar,
They sang to many a strange and distant shore.
                    And as the students came
And went, their minstrelsy was much the same,
Lives flowing like the waters as they pour.
The waters, rising from the sea, returned

To splash down from the rocky cliffs anew,
                    And living what they'd learned,
And finding life had proved the vision true,
The sons and daughters of the Alma Mater
                    Sent their children too,
So generations like the waters turned
In cycles ever old and ever new.
And all who came, before the falling water
At times that seemed abstracted out of time,
                    Would stand in wonder,
Hushed before your ceaseless rolling thunder,
And feel their spirits touched by thoughts sublime
For which words hardly ever could be found.
And so things went on like they always had
Until the fateful autumn rolled around.
For several days the weather had been bad.
The creek was high; behind the earthen wall
The forty-acre fishing lake was filled
With water waiting upstream from the Falls,
Waiting for its fate to be revealed.
                    While far below,
The campus waited, sleeping peacefully,
                    And did not know
What strange upheavals were about to be.

The story--you have heard it told before:
                    How the solid clay
Piece by piece began to wash away,
'Til through the dam the lake began to bleed--
How the trickle grew into a roar,
How o'er the Falls the water gathered speed--
How trees and trailers tossed like children's toys
                    Amidst the fearful noise--
How heroes struggled with amazing poise,
How many could do nothing else but pray--
How thirty nine would never see the day.

The story--you have heard it told before:
And how that marveling was turned to awe
                    When strangers saw
What joy and courage shone amidst the grief
And wondered where those left alive could draw
Such hope to carry on amidst the pain.
Meanwhile beneath the Falls, beside the shore,
Stronger even than they were before,
                    They still remain.

                    And still the waters pour
From sky to stream to sea to sky to stream,
And still they leap down from your rocky wall,
                    And as they fall,
They tease us into thoughts we cannot seem
To grasp--a vision glimpsed inside a dream.
And still we pose our questions--we are men,
And thus are doomed to ask, and ask again:
You bring us life and joy--you bring us woe,
Yet make us live the deeper by the blow;
You bring us blessing and you bring us pain,
Inextricably bound as by a chain--
As if there's no redemption but by blood--
                    And do we ask in vain?
What was the part that you played in the Flood?
Was something higher working for our good?
"Through fire and through water we have come
Into a wealthy place," the Psalmist said,
And we have quoted it, a rule of thumb
Which in some measure seems for us to sum
The path down which our history has led.
                    But is there something more?
Is the "Why?" a thing we can explore?
Are there causes raveled in a skein
                    That we can scan?
Was it just Nature's too-abundant rain?

Or was it part of some eternal plan?
Or was it anything we can explain?
It was the weakness of the works of Man.
                But is there something more?
Some meaning to the loss--and to the gain?
The fire and the water still remain.

                It never ceases.
The dead await their resurrection, and
                Their memory releases
The wisdom and the strength by which we stand.
And still your waters run, and in their flow
                One sometimes hears
Something like the music of the spheres--
The nearest thing to knowledge we can know
(Resonating with the surer Word
Of prophecy which from the Book is heard);
                Something we can trace
Of Power and of Suffering and of Grace;
Marching to it like a distant drum:
The closest to an answer we can come;
And somehow in our humble listening
We find that even we begin to sing
                (Oh joyful sound!)
A faint but faithful echo of the song
You sing, as playful as it is profound,
And having always as it rolls along
                One constant thesis:
Our Maker's face in grace and glory crowned.

                It never ceases.

ᔍ Epilogue ᔓ

Commentary, I Corinthians 13:12

The Southern Appalachians
In their autumn glory dressed
Are all the beauty we can bear,
Or in which we can rest.

The mighty hills of Heaven,
With their oppressive weight,
Would crush our spirits into dust,
Seen in our present state.

But when they burst upon us
In sudden majesty,
We will be given souls to match
And purer eyes to see.

ᔕ Book II ᘒ

The Seed
And Other Poems

"Dignus est Agnus, qui occisus est, accipere virtutem,

et divinitatem, et sapientam, et fortitudinem,

et honorem, et gloriam,

et benedictionem."

Ascriptions I

Shepherd of stars and winds and ocean waves,
Watcher of sparrows, Numberer of hairs,
Fierce Flinger forth of lightning flares,
Mountain Molder, Carver out of caves;
Smoke of Sinai, Setter free of slaves,
Grain Gatherer, Burner up of tares,
God alone who sees, alone who cares,
Life Giver, Opener of graves.

Our language lacks the necessary words,
Our minds the wit to sing your praise aright:
Inhabitor of hearts and vaulted naves,
Mighty Warrior, Healer, Lord who girds
His waist with righteousness, whose life is light:
God alone who sees, alone who saves.

Bereshith
Or, the Limits to the Explanatory Power
Of the Big-Bang Theory

In the beginning,
There was no time in which to locate time,
No winter moving toward a warmer clime,
Yet Something wound the clock and made it chime,
        Its dial forever spinning.

In the beginning,
There was no super-atom to explode,
No source from which its power could have flowed,
Yet Something put it there, supplied the goad,
        Its matter ever thinning.

In the beginning,
There was no space in which to locate space,
No place to move to from another place,
Yet Something started atoms on their race
        In stars forever spinning.

In the beginning,
What was it brought the universe to birth?
What force could make the heavens and the earth
And, saying they were good, could give them worth
        In the beginning?

Elementary

"And the world was without form and void, and darkness was upon the face of the deep. And the Spirit of God was brooding over the surface of the waters" (Gen. 1:2).

Earth, Water, Wind, and Fire
Each against the others strain
Until the stronger God, Desire,
Binds them in the Golden Chain.

Water, Wind, Fire, and Earth
Mix in Chaos uncontrolled
Until sweet Order, brought to birth,
Links them in the Chain of Gold.

Wind, Fire, Earth, and Water,
Each of which, in Nature's course,
Would make the world's foundations totter,
Bow before a greater Force.

Fire, Earth, Water, Wind
Perform what they've no knowledge of:
Find their unity and end
Within the Golden Chain of Love.

Harmony in universe,
From cacophony, a choir;
Thus does Grace redeem the curse
Of Earth, Water, Wind, and Fire.

Creation

Here's the marvel: that the self-contained
    And all-sufficient triple Unity
    Which for untold eternities had reigned
    Complete in his own pure simplicity
Should will unnecessary worlds to be.
    And yet his Mind was steel, his Purpose flint;
    He struck off sparks of flaming ecstasy,
    And called the stars by name. The thing He meant:
To make his Glory visible. He sent
    Forth pulsing space-time-matter-energy
    Which danced in pirouettes as on it went.
    Just one thing more was needed: eyes to see,
And skin to feel, and mind to comprehend.
    He called it Adam, and there made an end.

Four Preludes

"And the light shone in darkness and
Against the Word the unstilled world still whirled
About the center of the silent Word."

—T.S. Eliot, "Ash-Wednesday"

1

Thrice holy, three times spoken, meant, and heard
    By one voice speaking once, once only hearing,
    One only multifold, all-meaning Word
    From out of time, in time and flesh appearing;
Separate, though inseparably one,
    Thou who art not the Father, yet art God,
    Thou who art Son of Man, yet no man's son;
    Root of Jesse, Rock of Ages, Rod
Of Aaron blossoming in barren soil,
    Whose petals blades are of a burning sword
    Which strikes its deep wounds full of healing oil;
    Servant of all, and universal Lord;
With literal metaphors, we stumbling seek
    To praise Thee, strong firstborn of all who speak.

2

The void gulped down, but could not hold, the Word.
    The formless dark was shattered in a bright
    Explosion, flinging out across the night
A dancing host. As in a flock, each bird,
In answer to the music that is heard,
    Wheels in unison across the height
    Of Heaven, one, though many, in their flight,
Around the central Singer stars now whirred.
Giving voice to the unspoken Name
    That held them with strong bonds of pure desire,

Burning with reflected, holy flame,
  They showed forth unseen, sustaining fire.
  And still they sing. The Center which surrounds
    All circles still supplies their burning sounds.

3

His life lit up the world while yet the sun
    Was but an idea in her Maker's mind.
    Yet Lucifer the mighty looked upon
    His glory greedily, and was struck blind,
Inventing darkness of a different kind
    From what had been before. 'Til then, the night
    Had been left to contrast with that which shined,
    In pleasant patterns setting off the light
Which lit each angel's eyes and gave him sight.
    But now, light twisted into what was not,
    Swirled in perverse patterns, moved by spite,
    Was proclaimed as new vision, in a plot
To unseat God himself. The flaming Word
    Could not be quenched, but seeing eyes were blurred,

4

And self-willed pits of sightless blackness yawned
    Inside the minds of some. They screamed and fell
    Into themselves, pursuing a light that dawned
    Outside the Son, but all they found was Hell:
The self, clenched shut against the light, a shell
    Of utter loneliness where once had burned
    The singing fire, the holy flame, the well
    Of light reflected each to each, returned

To him who gave, received again, unearned,
    The gift: light which was love, love which was life;
    All this was that the falling angels spurned
    Because it was not of themselves. The strife
Which they began comes back to haunt mankind,
    Which likewise, seeking Sonless light, is blind.

Epilog

The Word in unchanged harmony still burns
At the world's heart. Around it slowly turns
A universe of self-inflicted pain.
Against our orbits, futilely, we strain
In grinding discord. For the blind depraved,
There's no escape but to be damned or saved.

Naming

And how he thought about them, trooping past,
  Stopping to lick his hand or sniff his knee--
  Tiny as a bee or hummingbird, or vast
  In girth the river-horse--and first to see
In fur and feather, clad heraldically,
  The colors--and the antics!--speechless, stare
  At scampering mice, at stallions' thunder, tree-
  Like limbs of elephants, ambling bulk of bear--
This creativity beyond compare--
  What fruit brought forth in bare but fertile mind;
  From sound and sight, throat muscles, subtle air,
  To weave the Words, the Poet's power unbind:
To call the Correspondences by name
  As Adam called the animals who came.

Earth

The origin and ground of all who grieve
    Is ground we walk on, kicking as we go
    The bones of Adam and the flesh of Eve.
Dust to dust, the day they took their leave
    They sowed the bitter seed of death and woe
    Deep in the fertile ground of all who grieve.
We reap the thorns and thistles, we receive
    The harvest, and within us still we grow
    The bones of Adam and the flesh of Eve.
With all our efforts, all we can achieve
    Is to extend the seedbeds, row on row,
    Planted in the ground of all who grieve.
The winds take up the dust, the winds that weave
    Their way around the world, and there they blow
    The bones of Adam and the flesh of Eve.
We look away; we'd rather not believe.
    Still, none who walks the earth can help but know
    The origin and ground of all who grieve:
The bones of Adam and the flesh of Eve.

"With Loss of Eden, 'Til One Greater Man..."

Eden recedes. A glooming darkness gathers
Over the spot where Abel's life-blood soaks
Into the ground. The growing family shatters.
Cain moves away, moves farther, breeds, and scatters
His seed. The spreading weed of darkness chokes
The light progressively. The story's tatters
Blow in a dark wind, flutter down the slopes
Of history, and blood cries out for blood.
So swords are forged, bows bent, and altars built.
Unceasingly the blood of Abel splatters
The dust we are until a sickening mud
Sucks at our feet. Pulled down into guilt,
We cling to altars with our bloody hands;
They cannot hold, and blood cries out for blood,
And still we try to answer blood's demands.
Poured into dust or splashed upon the stones,
It blackens as it thickens and it hardens.
Some of what splashed the altars was our own.
Impure, it makes our situation worse,
Leaves us only with more blood to pardon
As Eden recedes. We stumble through the night,
Torn by the thorns and thistles of the Curse,
Trying to find our way back to the Garden,
Hopeless our erring footsteps to reverse
As darkness grows and blood cries out for blood.

Epistle from the Limbo of the Righteous Pagans
(Cassandra Speaks)

We were very ignorant, but there were some things we knew.
We knew that life is a narrow Bridge of time,
That both ends lie beyond the sight of men,
And the fathomless abyss lies before, and behind, and beneath.
The rails on the Bridge are Morality and Custom,
And they are all that stand between us and Chaos.
Freedom is found only on the Bridge,
For there is no freedom in chaos and destruction.
We also tried to find the thing that you call freedom.
On the other side of the rails there is Nothing.
Would you also be free from earth, and sea, and sky?
Would you walk without the earth beneath your feet,
Breathe without air, swim without water?
Breath apart from air is suffocation:
Such is freedom from morality and custom.
So I say to you, get married and have children,
And teach them that doing right is the only thing that matters,
But that all the right they do will be insufficient
To cover all the wrong. This is why
The sacrificial blood must always flow.
We did not know from Whom it had to flow,
But the blood that splashed our altars was far wiser in its way
Than your sky-topping prayer-towers of glass and steel and
        concrete
Dedicated to the praise of perfectible Man.
Raise your children, then, and teach them,
Carefully and painfully,
By precept and example that freedom cannot be found
Elsewhere than in the man who does his duty,
Who is faithful unto death, though it be hard,
And then that even this is insufficient.
That was all the freedom we knew how to find.

I will not say that there is nothing better than this
(You perhaps have heard strange stories of a Hope we did not
        have),
But we tried also all the gods that you are looking to
And found them nothing, Nothing, dust
And ashes,
Dust and ashes.

Commentary,
Acts 17:23, Romans 1:23, Colossians 2:9

The ancients worshiped what they did not know:
        Corruptible men and beasts and creeping things
        Enthroned in splendor, deathless. From below,
        They scaled the sky with such imaginings,
But for that trip they needed stronger wings.
        The glimpses filled their hearts with holy dread;
        They could not see the way the King of kings
        Joined all the scattered hints into one Head:
Atropos, who snips thread after thread;
        Poseidon, master of the raging sea;
        Hera of the hearth and marriage bed;
        Live-giving power of Persephone;
Aphrodite's beauty; Ares' might;
        Zeus's thunder; and Apollo's light.

Irony

While the people fretted in their tents
And thought of garlic, then of leeks, and frowned,
And tried to sleep, and thought hard thoughts against
Old Moses, through the night, without a sound,
The golden manna gathered on the ground.

The "Murmuring Motif"

At the sea, the rushing waters stood;
    At Marah, bitter waters turned to sweet;
    At Meribah, it spurted from the rock.
The people saw and drank; it was as good
    As manna, honey-cakes they had to eat.
    They surely were a richly pastured flock.

Still, every time a little trouble came,
    Like starving goats, that flock began to bleat,
    And Moses had to listen to them mock.
If he thought that was the limit of their shame,
    He was in for a shock.

On David Writing the Psalms

Such words were never uttered unless by
Some battered brain's true trial- and tear-taught try
To cry the thing, heart's clearly seen lament
Before insight is wholly spent
Diffused, dispersed, immersed, and rent
By hurried passing Time.

Holy Spirit stooping, molding,
Prodding, soothing, moving, goading,
Guiding, forming in this writing
Sword or torch of Truth abiding,
Made to smite complacence in its nest,
To bore into the soul, unbidden guest,
And wake the wound that slumbers in man's breast:
A memory of the universe at rest.

The Cry:
Prophetic Fragment

I have walked the streets of cities and towns, and seen
The empty eyes disguised by endless laughter,
The blanker stares of men intent on business,
And over all the neon wash that drowns
The clean if scanty light of the evening sky,
        And a Voice said, "Cry!"
And I though, "What shall I cry?"
And so I read the lines of morning papers
And saw the cold statistics stacked in piles
Like countless bodies of aborted children
On the altars of the goddess Promiscuity,
        And the Voice said, "Cry!"
I listened to the sages of the people
On blaring, omnipresent radios,
And also read the words of learned poets,
        And they said,
"The frenzied freedom of the one-night stand
Is better than the faithful bonds of marriage,
And by all means don't get tied down with children.
If you feel that something's good, it is,
As long as it's not violent. Nobody
Is wise enough to tell you how to live,
And tolerance is the only virtue left,
And the only thing that's real's the present moment."
        And the Voice said, "Cry!"
I turned and to listen to the saints and preachers,
And they proclaimed that Man is very good
And has a spark of godhood deep within him.
And if somehow we just can fan that flame
With Education and Encounter Groups
And teach him to get over all his hang-ups
And to engage in honest self-expression,

The Evolution, Social Change, and Progress
Will make the world a place of peace and beauty.
     But the Voice said, "Cry!"
      And I said, "What shall I cry?
What word to heal the pain, explain the 'Why?'
What new solution we have yet to try,
What new direction for the race we run?"
     And the Voice said, "None.
You are to tell them that they have to die.
Tell them they cannot walk unless their feet are on the ground
Or know the Truth without rejecting lies.
Say there is no freedom to be found
     In throwing away all ties.
Say that we must choose our metaphors
(And mix them) carefully, if we would see
The signs above the doors
     And take the right road to eternity."

That road is harder for the man who thinks that he is rich;
The blind inevitably lead the blind into the ditch.
The ditch is deep (it splits the world asunder)
And wider than the space between the stars;
And there it waits for man the way the lightning waits for
     thunder,
     Or wounded flesh for scars.

Revelation: Natural, Special
Commentary, Romans 1:18-23, 2:14-16

Inscribed upon the stars and in our bones
    Is truth we know so well and yet suppress.
    The hardest tablets are not made of stone.
In spite of all we say that we condone,
    Conscience whispers softly nonetheless
    Of Laws within the stars and in our bones.
We drown the Voice with chatter; on we drone.
    It calls us back, but still we will digress:
    The hardest tablets were not made of stone.
When Moses climbed the Mountain all alone,
    A Finger into slabs of rock impressed
    What stood upon the stars and in our bones.
Before he could get back, they would be thrown
    To break against the flint within our breasts:
    The hardest tablets were not made of stone.
Part of Creation's universal groan,
    The Voice will not be stilled, for still it rests
    Inscribed upon the stars and in our bones:
The hardest tablets are not made of stone

Why God is to be Worshipped

"God is a Circle whose center is everywhere and whose circumference is nowhere."
– Traditional Definition

"I am like the center of a circle equidistant from all points on the circumference, but you are not."
– Love, in Dante's *Vita Nuova*

He is pure Light without a hint of turning
    Or shadowed spot.
He is pure Vision, perfectly discerning
    Which from what.
He is pure Holiness, forever spurning
    Stain or blot.
He is pure Love. Our story from His yearning
    Derives its plot.
He is pure Might, whose will cannot be hindered
    By rebel plot.
He is a Sphere whose every point is centered,
    And we are not.

Martyres

"On the evidence of two or three witnesses every matter shall be confirmed" --Deuteronomy. 19:15b

I

Anthropos

"And yet He did not leave Himself without witness, in that He did good and gave you rains from heaven and fruitful seasons, satisfying your hearts with food and gladness."

–Acts 14:17

"Therefore, having overlooked the times of ignorance, God is now declaring to men that all everywhere should repent because He has fixed a day in which He will judge the world in righteousness through a Man whom He has appointed, having furnished proof to all men by raising Him from the dead."

–Acts 17:30-31

We sensed that there was something. In the sky
It somehow seemed to be, or in the wind —
A Voice, a subtle message in the dew,
Something in our hearts that would not lie
Quiet when we knew that we had sinned.
(How did we know that it was sin? We knew.)

Something. Power hidden in the earth
To push the blades and buds up in the spring.
At first we gave each face of it a name;
So sky and field and river each gave birth
To its own god, and men began to bring
The blood they shed to cover up their shame.

And they did right, though they did not know why
Until the Voice called out to Abraham
To leave his father for an unknown land.
A cave for burial he had to buy,
A mountain-thicket where he found a ram,
Sore feet, the burning sun, and blowing sand,

More mysteries than answers he could learn,
A son to whom he could bequeath the trial,
An oath, but not one acre he could claim
Were all that wanderer got in return—
Plus one thing more that made it all worthwhile:
He saw through all that flickers to the Flame.

And so his seed would bear the message, "Hear
Oh Israel, the Lord your God is One!"
And camp at Sinai when the Flame came down.
Though all too easily the holy fear
Engendered by the way they had begun
Was lost, at least they got their piece of ground.

And there they stayed, and there they read the Law,
And studied, and debated every word,
And kept alive at least some memory
Of who they were and what their fathers saw.
But what the Flame had shown, the smoke had blurred,
And most of them would finally fail to see

The Thing they'd waited for through all those years,
The Something we had groped for in our fears.
The hopes, the blood, the altars—who'd have guessed
That this would be the answer to our quest?
The smoke of Sinai slowly cleared away
To show a Baby lying in the hay.

II
Angelos

"And suddenly an angel of the Lord stood before them and the glory of the Lord shone round about them, and they were sore afraid. And the angel said unto them, "Do not be afraid; for behold, I bring you good tidings of great joy which shall be to all people. For unto you this day in the City of David is born a Savior, who is Christ, the Lord. And this shall be a sign unto you: you will find the baby wrapped in swaddling clothes and lying in a manger. And suddenly there was with the angel a multitude of the heavenly hosts, praising God and saying, "Glory to God in the highest, and on earth, peace, good will toward men."

--Luke 2:9-14

"It was revealed to [the prophets] that they were not serving themselves, but you, in these things which now have been announced to you through those who preached the Gospel to you by the Holy Spirit sent from heaven—things into which angels long to look."

--1 Peter 1:12

We were the first of all His thoughts to live
And know ourselves as living in His Mind,
And that was all the world we'd ever known.
Pure thought He made us, and to each would give
Great visions of rare creatures he'd designed.
The strangest? Thought conjoined with flesh and bone.

We took it as a kind of abstract game,
An intellectual and eternal dance.
Imagine then our wonder and delight
When He spoke, and the whole expanding frame
Of space unfolded 'round us, and, entranced,
We saw the ideas made and loved the sight!

Then, more than that, He gave us jobs to do
And, as we'd shared His thoughts, we shared His work:

To form our dance of ideas into things.
As swift as thought at His behest we flew,
Taking the light He'd made into the mirk
Of space and time, the light itself our wings.

Not all of us together knew it all.
According to our stature He would share
With each some insight, but the larger plan
Remained a source of wonder. Still, one small
World of all we made was our chief care,
For there He made His masterpiece: the Man.

Though we were pure intelligence, we caught
So little of the grandeur of His Mind!
He'd brought forth thought in us; we'd seen Him bring
Forth space-time filled with things beyond our thought;
But we thought nothing that He did outshined
His strange idea of Man, a thinking thing.

But then the whole plan seemed to go awry.
Our brother Lucifer loved the mastery
Of things more than he did the One who gave
It to us, and his thought became a lie.
And then, when Adam joined him at the Tree,
Our joy fell into dust, into the grave.

We thought it was the end, but we were wrong,
For then, the greatest marvel! How we long
To look into it still—we raced to sing
The "Gloria!"—if we'd thought the strangest thing
Was thinking flesh, then what else could we say
About *that* Baby lying in the hay?

Bethlehem

Bethlehem, *Beth Lechem*, House of Bread:
    Your white stones waited silent in the sun
    For long years (long as people feel them run).
The prophets wrote no more; the Rabbis read
The old words and unraveled every thread
    And found your secret out: you were the one.
    And when the time came and the thing was done,
They spent the night at home asleep in bed.

Oh, they could put their fingers on the pages
    That told the old fox Herod it was you.
But those uncircumcised, stargazing sages
    Came first, and shepherds, wet with evening dew,
Had long since been there, and all had been fed
    In Bethlehem, *Beth Lechem*, House of Bread.

Oh Sight Beyond All Seeing

Oh Sight beyond all seeing,
Light in the dark of the sun,
Fact behind the face of Being,
Second of Three in the One:
What motive could have moved you hither thus?
The Life that was ever begotten, never begun,
Began to be born, to mourn. For us
The daring deed was done.

Burned by Angel-light,
The shepherds' eyes were blind
To everything except the sight
That they went forth to find.
It was a baby wrapped in swaddling clothes,
Laid in a manger: such had been the sign.
The sign they saw by then still shows
The perilous paths that wind

Between the Tree and the Tree.
This much the sign makes clear:
The Light invisible we see,
The silent Word we hear.
What motive could have moved him hither thus?
We hear pegs pounded, see the thrusted spear,
We hear, "Forgive them!" Now for us
The day of doom draws near.

The Seed

I
Overview

The dog cried out with the voice of a man suffering,
Low and hoarse, the throat tense and hollow;
Never before, that cry, and never since,
And then but once with the first one--afterwards, silence.
My hand on her head, accepted but not acknowledged,
The brown eyes focused on something beyond us both--
Then licking, breaking of membranes, puppies breathing,
No luck with the nipples at first, but soon sucking,
The hand acknowledged now, the eyes tired.
Six puppies and I don't know how many hours
Were born in the time of releasing a single sigh.

For the woman it was one child only, but more hours:
Twenty-one in the room with the tubes and passing nurses,
My hand on her shoulder, accepted and acknowledged,
The hazel eyes focused on a spot on the far wall
To foster concentration on the rhythms,
The breathing we'd practiced and practiced to ward off pain;
Looking through the spot, searching for something
That had flashed in the sad brown eyes six months before.
From the room next door there came the sounds of groaning,
The woman's voice unmistakable, low and hoarse,
The throat tense and hollow, the voice of the beagle.

My woman would let no cry escape, but panted,
And finally simply said, "I cannot do this!"
Then, past all waiting, hoping, and despairing,
The child was there, alive, slimy, crying,
And I said, "What in the world are we going to do now?"
And she smiled weakly, "Take her home and love her."

And I wonder how it was for Eve the first time,
In a tent or a cave outside the walls of Eden
With no one to tell her, "It will be like this."
For she would be the first who would remember,
The first to find the words to help another.
But now there was only Adam, shaking and helpless,
And Eve, shaking and shaken, the blood pounding
Her head with the words remembered and carried from Eden,
The Strife of the Seed and the Serpent, the Hope of the Bruising.
And then she felt it: the Serpent constricting to kill her!
She bellowed defiance, her hands clenched white in the skin
Of the beast that the furious Jahweh had killed for a covering:
This above all she would cling to, pass on to her daughters.
She whispered to Adam, "I've gotten a man from the Lord."

And the years passed, and the seed strove with the darkness,
And Eden became a memory, faint and painful,
And men strove to forget, and some succeeded,
And the waters rose and fell, and Noah came through them,
And the Tower rose and fell, and the peoples were scattered,
And then there was Sarah, old and toothless and laughing,
But her laughter died in a pain that was old as Eve.
And Ruth lay down and uncovered the feet of Boaz,
And knew not what was at stake (and yet, she knew),
 And David wore the crown, sweet singer of Israel.
There were twenty-eight generations from David to Mary.

And Mary was a young girl far from home,
And the best that Joseph could do for her was a stable,
And her time came, and only the shepherds knew it.
That night the sword pierced her heart for only the first time,
And the first and the last were alike, the birth and the death:
The pain, then the life, the death, then the resurrection,
The seed's heel bruised again, the head of the Serpent
Finally crushed. She pondered the sword in her heart,
The wheat falling and dying, the fruit brought forth

(For the light shines from an empty tomb in Jerusalem,
And childbirth itself was made that that might be),
The pain and the joy, life, the song and the sorrow.

The years that have passed have given us things to remember.
I remember the hand on the head, the silky ears,
The brown eyes wide with surprise, but patient, waiting;
Then later the hand on the woman's side, guided
By her's, from the depths within, the foot, kicking.
I remember the shoulders under my hands, the cold sweat.
I look at my daughter now, running and playing,
Squealing with joy, stooping to pat the beagle,
And think, when she is older I will tell her,
"We strive still, the woman's seed, with the darkness,
Though all strive to forget, and some succeed,
But my first sight of you there with your mother
Will help me remember, make me think and remember
 The cost to the woman, the cost to the Seed of the Woman."
Perhaps the words will be with her when her time comes;
Her mother will read them now, and understand.

II
Campfire Tale

"I will tell you a story.
It is a true story; I did not make it up.
I learned it word for word from the way the words
Followed each other like first stars in the dark
When they came to me the first time, long ago.
I am still learning it.
And though it grows in the telling, it does it the way
A seed grows into a cedar, because the cedar
Was there in the seed all along, and had to grow.
You can find them tall and majestic in the fields,
Daring the lightning, or stooped, twisted, stunted,
Clutching at some impossible crack in a rock,
Living on soil they had to grind themselves,

But living to scatter their seed.
You are hearing the story from me; I am telling it now.
The seeds ride on the wind. If I should stop,
Sooner or later one would take root near you;
You find them growing in unexpected places.
I will tell you a story."

"The story has no beginning, but we will start
With a cold night in the desert, the stars fierce,
A light wind stirring the sand, the hints of dawn
As yet too faint to challenge the blazing blackness.
There is no moon tonight; you must look closely.
You see that hill? It seems to be moving. Ha!
It is a tent collapsing. There are camels
Kneeling to be loaded. I hear bleating
Of sheep. And there, that man off to the side,
He seems oblivious to the whole commotion,
Standing motionless against the sky
As if in meditation. One of the servants
Approaches him now, but stops, patiently waiting.
That man must be the master here. He sees
The servant, sighs, and turns back toward the others.
I've lost him, but he must be mounted now;
There go the camels, lurching, one by one,
Rising clumsily into the sky.
And now they're moving. What a host they've got!
How could we have missed those flocks? They're gone.
Before the sun is up the wind will sweep
Away all signs that they were ever here."

The boy stared deep in the fire. "You tell it as if
You were there when it happened, as if it were happening
        now."

"And how do you know it isn't?" The old man's eyes
Glinted. He shoved a stick in deeper and made

The sparks fly up. "The story is still going on,
And you and I are in it. The man was traveling
With everything he owned, cattle, servants,
Their wives and children, deeper into the desert.
 None of them knew where they were going or why.
His wife had asked him point-blank, and he had told her
That God had told him to go, and that was that.
Some of them even believed him!" The light of the fire
Showed a smile that wrinkled the old man's cheeks
At that point. "Yes, there were some of them that believed
        him."

The old man paused 'til the boy thought he'd fallen asleep,
But then he shook his head. "It is not to be thought
That the man knew fully himself why the journey was ordered.
He thought it had something to do with becoming a nation.
The begetting of seed was central in it somehow,
And some great blessing for all mankind was at stake.
He thought it had something to do with the Curse and the
        Promise
Of Eden, the Seed that was coming to bruise the Serpent."

"So that old story's the same as this one?"
                                          "Yes.
There is only one story you know. But all he knew
Was that Jahweh had told him to leave Ur of the Chaldees
And God had promised a land and a seed and a blessing."

This time it was the boy who stirred the fire.
"And did he ever find the land he was seeking?"

The old man laughed. "Well, we are here now, aren't we?"

"And did he find the seed?"

                                    The old man's hand
Descended gently on the boy's young shoulder.

"The story goes no further for tonight.
We'd better get some sleep now, for tomorrow
We'll come to the place appointed for sacrifice.
 Tomorrow night we may know more of the story,
And if we do we'll tell it to each other."

The fire was watchful beside them through the night,
And the silent tears of Abraham were tiny
Pools of mud in the dust by the sleeping form
Of Isaac, the promised seed. It was a cold
Night on the edge of the desert, the stars fierce,
The hints of dawn still faint, but growing stronger,
A light wind stirring the thicket where the ram
Had gotten himself entangled on the mountain.

III

The Moment

The seed had slept some fourteen years, but now
There was more than silent darkness: something new,
A gentle motion, growing warmth. Somehow
The tiny cell knew what it had to do:
Glide on and be receptive to its fate,
Either a greater change, or death. The girl
Felt nothing whatsoever when the weight
That counterpoises all the blazing swirl
Of suns we call the universe was pressed
To needle concentration down and driven
Into her belly. She could not have guessed
The power of the gift so softly given;
The egg would never be the same again.
It would have been annihilated by
The impact if the same force had not been
 Within, sustaining. Men who watched the sky
Were startled by a star they did not know;
The demons trembled, and did not know why;
In Mary's womb, the Seed began to grow.

IV
The Carpenter's Son

He loved to watch his father work the wood:
To take the rough timber, plane it smooth,
Lay out the lines and cut and join, and soon
A table, bed, or chest would stand before you.
The boy could hardly speak in sentences
As yet, but he could think, and what he thought
Was more than Milton could have found the words for.
Every movement summoned up for him
Sights he'd never seen, but still remembered:
From father's simple angles surged a swirl
Of spheres moving in concentric circles,
Frightening in complexity and speed
But pure and elegant in symmetry,
In ratios recognized but left unnamed--
The scraping of the plane was wind and water,
Incessant singing of the sea and air,
The slow grinding of suspended dust--
He ran his hand along the grain and felt
The tree's intensity in lifting water
To leaves, turning sunlight into sugar,
All to fuel its joy in raising branches
 To Heaven in praise of ...and he felt the praise.
He was not ready even yet to name
This knowledge that the wood had brought to him.
He felt it shudder in his hands, recalling
Axe-blows to its roots as living tree,
And clenched it tight until it pained his palms
And forced the sweat in beads out on is forehead,
And thought of nothing else until his father
Told him gently, "Son, it's time for supper."

He was merry again at meat, and made them laugh;
But later when they'd tucked him into bed,
They climbed up on the roof to feel the cool

Peace of evening as the stars came out.
In muffled tones that mingled joy and worry
They talked awhile, turning over the thing
That had come to them to try and see it clearly.
The stars helped, reminding them of the night
When all had seemed so plain: the birth-joy, pure
Shared with the shepherds, unalloyed by pain,
The hope of help from Heaven for their people
Realized at last. Then too, he'd seemed
So small and helpless, just like all the other
Newborns they had held--nieces, nephews.
It was easy to believe he was really theirs,
And that was happiness enough. The hard
Words of Gabriel, "Over-shadowed ...Holy . . .
Yeshuah ...Savior ...King," were for the future
Or the past. For now, let's just enjoy him!
It was not to be. The eighth day, journey,
Jerusalem, the time for circumcision:
"That crazy old man in the Temple
Who came right up and took him from my arms,
Do you remember?"
                              "How could I forget?
As if we didn't have enough to ponder.
'A light of revelation to the Gentiles,'
He said, and what they have to do with it
I'd like to know!"
                              "It's in Isaiah."
                                             "Maybe.
But let him see to his own people first,
I say."
           "But Joseph, Joseph, you're forgetting
The worst part. He's appointed for the fall
Of many within Israel, and a sign
To be opposed--and that about the sword!"

"I know. And if there's any pain to be

Inflicted in all this, he'll bear the brunt.
I see it in him now, and that's the worst.
Last Friday in the shop I cut my hand--
You'd thought I'd cut his heart to see his face--
And he came up and asked if he could take it.
I thought he meant my hand. He took the pain!
I mean, he took it, not just to discard it--
He absorbed it somehow, and he held it
For just a moment, and then it was gone."

"Yes, I know. He does that. But remember
 When we got back and finally found that house,
Those strange men from the East. Now, they were
        Gentiles,
And called him king of Jews, but worshiped him
As if he were their own."
                              "And brought him presents."
"Yes. Do you remember what the third one
Said when he had laid his coffer down?"

'"'He will have need of this.' And when we opened
It up it was completely full of myrrh."

"Embalming spice!"
                      "I don't know what it means.
I don't know what he means. I don't know anything
Except he makes me sad and glad together
'Til I can hardly tell the two apart."

"Maybe it has to be that way awhile
So that the joy can win out in the end."

"If that is so, the pain will triumph first.
You mark my words."
                        "Yes, that's what I'm afraid of."

- 130 -

The starlight was too dim to show the pair
An answer to their questions, and almost
Too dim to show them going down to bed.
But it kept shining after they were gone
On a band of shepherds somewhere to the south
And three old wizards hidden in the east
Who were occupied with questions of their own.

V
The Knowledge

The knowledge slept inside him like a seed.
Sometimes he felt it opening, putting down
Its roots into his soul, or sending up
Tentative feelers toward the conscious mind.
His appetite for learning was voracious:
It always felt more like remembering,
As if he knew all things somewhere deep down,
But could not think them 'til he met with something
In this strange world of sight and sound and texture
To give them substance, clothe them with a form
Which tongue and lips could grasp and turn to sound.

The Word unheard and those he learned for speaking
Moved toward each other in the throbbing
Darkness just behind his consciousness;
A Light beyond the sight of mortal men,
But one he sensed, was there--and all his thoughts,
Like moths flitting on a summer evening,
Kept circling toward that light and what it meant.

The roots sank deeper and the shoots pushed upward.
Lilies bloomed in the fields and the birds flew,
Summer and winter, seedtime and harvest came,
Wheat died and was buried and brought forth fruit,
Men haggled over it in the market,

And Mary kneaded leaven into the dough.
All these things worked like leaven in his spirit
To swell the growing knowledge of who he was.

The strangeness of it never quite wore off:
To know all things and yet to have to learn,
To have to sort things out and search for truth--
If anything, it grew as he grew older
And the seed began to sprout and put forth leaves.

"Tell me again--what did the angel say
The day he told you that I would be coming?
Was he the same the shepherds saw? I wonder."
Meshiach, the Anointed, throne of David,
Yeshuah, save his people from their sins,
Immanuel, God with us: all she told him
Was like the spring rain and the summer sun.
He began to recognize his Father's voice
(Like, and yet unlike, the voice of Joseph)
In those few phrases, like a little child
Who cannot understand the words, but gets
The tone, full of authority and love.
Both tone and words sank deep into the soil
To feed and form the quickly growing plant.

He was put to school at the synagogue to learn
That words were made of sounds, and sounds had
        shapes
That could be put down on paper or skin and kept,
And made back into words again at will.
Now he read the Torah for himself.
The Father's voice was unmistakable:
The rain splashed on the leaves, the sun was warm,
And the roots dug in and fruit began to form.
The Woman was promised a seed, and Abel was killed,
And then the seed was Abraham's, and Isaac

Climbed the mountain and asked, "Where is the ram?"
And had to climb the altar to get his answer.
Moses' bush was lit with the fire that burned
In the boy's own bones without consuming them;
Pharaoh's stubbornness only stoked the flames
Until they did consume his firstborn son.
Israel journeyed swiftly with their sons,
But every family left with one lamb less.
The Fire came down again, and Sinai smoked.
A pillar of fire by night, a cloud by day;
Forty scapegoats scattered through the desert,
And every year the bull was brought, and every
Year they had to bring it once again.

This year it would be brought, and he would be there;
Son of the Covenant, he would make the trip
And see the City where the prophets suffered.
The flame that burned the bush and left it standing,
The fire that fueled the sun and kept it burning,
That roared from Sinai to dispel the darkness,
That flamed behind his mind and lit his way,
That burned inside the seed and forced it open,
That was the light of the world, the life of men,
Yet would destroy them if not cooled with blood,
Burned low before the altar in the Temple
And called him with a voice that was his own.
One question yet must come into its light:
Seed of the Woman, Seed of Abraham--
If such a seed were planted, what would grow?
A bush aflame with love and holiness,
A light of revelation to the Gentiles,
Of course. But that same light had shone before,
And men loved darkness. How could it burn brighter?
How would he justify the angel's naming:
Yeshuah, savior of his people from

Their sins, not Rome or Babylon. And this time,
In what wild thicket would the ram be found?

The ceremonies themselves were disappointing.
You couldn't really see, and all the people
Were rough and noisy--hardly seemed to think
Of what was going on or why. The Temple
Was grand, but really only just a building,
Just one stone on another after all.
The Shekinah was long departed, and in its place
Were things that did not satisfy at all:
Moneychangers, sheep, birds in cages.
The fire burned in the corners of his eyes,
But he held his peace until his time was come.

Meanwhile there was one thing that held his interest:
In the portico the learned rabbis
Gathered to hold discourse with their disciples
And any others who might seek their wisdom.
The Father's voice was faint, a far-off echo,
Like words passed through too many mouths until
They come out scrambled. Even that compelled him
And drew him like a magnet. For awhile
He listened quietly and did not speak.
Then suddenly the Father's voice cut sharply,
Like a sword. One of the sages took
A large scroll and carefully unrolled it;
One of the prophets the boy had not yet read.

"For he shall grow up like a tender plant,
A root from dry ground ...we esteemed him not.
Surely he hath born our griefs and carried
Our sorrows. He was wounded--bruised--chastised
For our transgressions and iniquities,
And like a lamb to slaughter he was led."

And time stood still for him, and there was only
The Word and how it echoed in his soul.
"Who is this Servant, and when will he come?"
The rabbis knew what everyone had said
For half a thousand years about the subject,
But never seemed to get down to the answer.
And then his parents came, and he was shocked
To know he'd put them through three days of worry.
"I had to be about my Father's business,"
Was all the explanation he could offer,
And it hurt to know they could not understand.
Then on the long walk home to Nazareth
They worried that he seemed preoccupied.
He was. The trunk was growing stout and strong,
Though still the leaves were tender, and the roots
Were beginning to feel the dryness of the ground.
He would be merry again, but for awhile
He wept like Jeremiah, and his parents
Chafed at their inability to help him.

Seed of the Woman, Seed of Abraham--
If such a seed were planted, what would grow?
He knew he was beginning at last to know.

VI
The Seed

And so the Seed was planted, and it grew.
And though it seemed an ordinary tree,
The Gardener knew what it was to do.

That every kind of bird that ever flew
Should nest upon its limbs was the decree,
And so the Seed was planted, and it grew.

Though any reason why it should be true
Was more than men as yet had eyes to see,
The Gardener knew what it was to do.

Although the soil was dry, and rocky too,
The branches spread out strong and green and free:
And so the Seed was planted and it grew.

If growth so rich could be left to accrue--
But that was not the way it was to be;
The Gardener knew what it had to do.

Chop it down, a lifeless stump? And who
Could see hope in such heartless husbandry?
But so the Seed was planted, and it grew:
The Gardener knew what He had to do.

Reflections

From the initial moment of surprise
    By piercing light they never had expected,
    The Magi mulled the meaning of the skies.
Was the betrayal worse, or were the lies?
    What in her swelling belly he'd detected
    Joseph couldn't find in Mary's eyes,
And that was puzzling. Puzzling to the Wise
    Men were their stumbling thoughts as they reflected
    Deeply on the meaning of the skies.
Joseph made them gentle, his good-byes,
    Turned sadly from the girl he had selected,
    Still haunted by the tears that filled her eyes.
Who knows what led those scholars to surmise
    The answer to the problem they'd dissected
    And journey toward the meaning of the skies?
An angel and his faith made Joseph prize
    The woman he had earlier rejected.
    The Magi mulled the meaning of the skies,
But Joseph saw the Star in Mary's eyes.

The Irony

The shepherds had no word for paradox
    (A learned term), but scratching of the head
    Was something that they knew, and as they sped
Toward Bethlehem, abandoning their flocks,
And stumbling in their haste upon the rocks,
    They did some over what the angel'd said:
    Messiah in a manger for a bed?
A king whose courtiers were ass and ox?

Perhaps the biggest part of the surprise
    Was that they were the ones who should be told:
    This savior did not seem to fit the mold
Constructed by the Mighty and the Wise.
    To stable smells and angels' caroling,
    Condemned and incognito came the King.

The Hypostatic Union

The Word set forth before the world began
    Wrote out the mournful tune in minor key:
    The crying of the infant Son of Man.
There was no way that they could understand
    How that small and helpless child could be
    The Word set forth before the world began.
Joseph wondered at the tiny hand,
    The scrunched-up face, the frail intensity
    Of crying in the infant Son of Man.
The angel host deployed and took its stand
    To sing out with celestial harmony
    The Word set forth before the world began.
Mary marveled at the shepherd band
    Who came to hear, while bowing awkwardly,
    The crying of the infant Son of Man.
Yet it was in accordance with the plan
    Articulated from eternity:
    The Word set forth before the world began
Was crying in the infant Son of Man.

Christmas Question

"Mary, did you know?" the carol asks.
　　　　The answer is not simple. She could tell
　　　　The meaning of the name Immanuel,
But the true nature of Messiah's tasks
Was hid. A multiplicity of masks,
　　　　Their messianic expectations fell
　　　　Across their anxious eyelids like a veil.
Still, hidden in an alabaster flask,

The precious perfume of the Promise, kept
　　　　So carefully until the destined hour
　　　　About which all the prophecies had spoken,
Was moving with the Magdalene, who wept,
　　　　Whose tears fell with the ointment in a shower
　　　　On Feet that for her sins would soon be broken.

Soliloquy: The Shepherd

I was never before a man of many words.
What I had to say could be expressed
In curses mumbled at the wayward herds
Or loudly shouted at the boys from town.
The buyers of mutton might just be addressed
Not much more civilly, as up and down
We haggled over whether I would die
Of hunger or live yet another year.
The sky at night was simply the night sky,
A thing to be ignored. I knew to fear
Then only hunger and the hungry wolf.

I've learned a lot since those days of both fear
And hunger, and had more of both than ever.
There was no moon that night, and yet the stars
Shone with a light the like of which I'd never
Seen before. Not since I was a child
Had I taken notice of the way their light
On a clear, frosty night, out in the wild,
Can fill you up with hunger--no, with fright--
Well, something else that's both, and yet is neither.
They'd seemed then like a thousand eyes, whose sight
Could see clean through a man and leave no secrets.
Their piercing gaze had never bored as deep
As it did on that night. They seemed so near!
I told myself it was just lack of sleep,
That they could not be really getting closer.
But as I tried to explain that to the sheep,
The endless blackness which is seen to lie
Between the stars to keep them separate
Was in a moment squeezed out of the sky,
And I was knocked flat on m y face by light
That thundered like the sea--or by a choir

Of voices that shone brighter than the sun,
And burnt me to the bone with searing fire.

I'd always joked that when Messiah came
I'd ask him what he meant to do about
The price of sheep. If that was not his game,
I'd know he was a Christ of no concern
To me. But I was in no way prepared
For angels, with their messages that burn
Behind them after they are gone, and drive
You down the dark, deserted roads at night
To see a baby lying in the hay.
Still less was I prepared for such a sight
As that was. Yes, he had to do with sheep
Alright (the Lamb of God the prophets called him!),
And with their price. The one he paid was steep:
It was himself, and I purchased the sheep.

Of course, I didn't find that out 'til later.
That night I only knew I was afraid,
And hungry for I knew not what. But listen!
I've seen forty summers bloom and fade
Since then, and I would rather know that fear
Than all the ease that Caesar now enjoys
In his bright palace. Soon--perhaps this year--
I go to join my fathers, hungry still
With an eternal hunger. But the bread
I found that night in Bethlehem will fill
Me then as earthly meat has not. I am
Invited to the Supper of the Lamb!

Temptation

"And if the Voice at Jordan really said
 That you were his beloved Son, when on
 Your shoulder came the Spirit--you need bread?
 Just ask! He'd make a loaf for you from stone.
Now, you were sent to take—I'll not say 'steal'--
 The kingdoms over which I rightly reign.
 I'm not unreasonable. Let's make a deal:
 No need for either of us to suffer pain.
Salvation's (as you know) by faith. Let's make
 It easy for the people to believe.
 It says right in the Bible you'll not break
 A bone, so jump! The angels will receive ..."
Thrice, "No!" The only answer Satan heard:
 Three times, the simple power of the Word.

The Call

The sunlight danced upon the sand,
The breakers leaped across the shore.
The fisherman's heavy, calloused hand
Clenched the net until it tore,
For he was troubled by Prophet's lore.
The stranger spoke of life and death.
His words were like a salty breath
Of sea-wind on a sun-baked day;
The fisherman reddened, looked away,
And doubted not the truth, but yet the man.
Why should this queer wandering stranger
Seek him out to tell of danger?
He knew not what he stood to gain,
Nor clearly what he stood to lose.
He did not know--yet it was plain
He'd shortly have to choose.
"Leave your nets and come!" He heard him say.
The stranger walked away . . .

The Professionals
(Commentary, Luke 5:5)

"We've toiled all night and caught no fish as yet;
    Our eyes are drooping and our muscles ache.
    But at your bidding, we'll let down the net."
(Though, just 'twixt you and me, I doubt we'll get
    A single tug at this end of the lake.
    We've toiled all night and caught no fish as yet.)
"A better preacher we have never met,
    But teaching us to fish? That takes the cake!
    Still, at your bidding we'll let down the net."
(I don't know why we're doing this. I'll bet
    He's never fought this hard to stay awake.
    We've toiled all night and caught no fish as yet.)
And yet, somehow I don't think we'll regret
    Obeying him, though seaweed's all we'll take.
    So, "At your bidding we'll let down the net."
Then, without warning, every line was set
    So taut we were afraid that it would break:
    We'd toiled all night and caught no fish as yet,
But, at his bidding, we let down the net.

Soliloquy: The Samaritan Woman

I didn't expect, that day, to find him there,
His tired legs stretched out along the ground--
For I'd come late, just to avoid the stares,
The winks, the giggled whispers, and the frowns
Of all the other women of the town.

I didn't expect to find him there that day,
His weary back propped up against the well
(For the burdens of the whole world seemed to weigh
Upon his mighty shoulders), but we fell
To talking. Who he was, I could not tell.

But he could tell me everything that I
Had ever done. His words into the core
Of my soul struck and burned and made me cry.
And I, who'd known so many men before,
Could I dare think that he was something more?

A prophet, surely. You could see he knew
Things that no ordinary man could know.
And when he spoke of God, his words rang true
As if he knew firsthand that they were so.
"I know Messiah's coming, and he will show

Us all things when he comes," I said, and he
Gave me a look that made my heart stand still
In wonder, fear, and awed expectancy
To hear what he would say. His words were chill,
Like a drink from the mountain-high spring that refreshes
and fills!

And all that he said was, "I am He."
I ran back to the town to tell the rest,
"Messiah is at the well--Oh, come and see!"
Some stared at me as if I were possessed,
Or the maker (or brunt, perhaps) of some bad jest,

But some there were who did come back with me
To my new master, Jesus, there to be
From all their load of sin and self set free.

Fishers of Men

Two boats of fish, crammed to the gunwales, full:
    A week of work accomplished in one day!
    Yet it exerted hardly any pull.
    We left them in the sun and walked away.
We had to follow Him. How could we stay?
    He'd called the fish into our nets, and then
    He called to us. You ask, what did He say?
    Just, "Come! From now on, you will fish for men."
To doubt He was the Christ would be a sin.
    There was no way we should have caught those fish!
    But there they were, with gill and scale and fin,
    As many and as big as we could wish.
But, this man-fishing: What's that all about?
    I've got a feeling we will soon find out.

In Short

The fullness of ages,
The smell of the hay;
The gifts of the Sages,
The dawning of day.

The river of Jordan,
The Voice from above;
The weight of the Burden,
The wing of the Dove.

The test of temptation,
The talk on the hill;
The waves' inundation,
The lake water still.

The dough and the leaven,
The one missing sheep;
The treasure in Heaven,
The harvest to reap.

The tale for the mind,
The fishes, the bread;
The light of the blind,
The life of the dead.

The mountain of Zion,
The statement, "I Am!"
The heart of the Lion,
The blood of the Lamb.

Conversion
(Commentary, Luke 5:27-28)

Who would have thought old Levi would be able
To leave that money lying on the table?
He wasn't, until Jesus changed his mind;
He was not able then to stay behind!

Miracula

It is not so astounding that a stone
Would have cried out, "Hosannah!" had the crowd
Left the Lord to enter town alone.
More marvel you can read these lines aloud:
      In us
    He gave a tongue to dust.

It is not so amazing that he meant
To purchase all our sorrow for his own
And for that painful bargain to have spent
The Glory at the right hand of his throne:
      His love
    Him to such deeds would move.

But ponder this for paradox: the ones
To whom that gift was given--life complete,
Eternal peace, adoption as his sons!--
With such ingratitude can daily treat
      As worthless toys
    Such high and holy joys.

Commentary, Luke 19: 41

The crowds cried out "Hosannah!"
As his humble mount drew near.
The waving of the branches,
The excitement of the cheers,
The strewing of their garments
Kept their thoughts from being clear;
But the Savior saw the City
And saluted it with tears.
Still they echo through the years!

Eucharist

Once again the Lord of Heaven
Stoops with towel around His waist,
Breaks the Bread made without leaven,
Watches Judas leave in haste.

Once again the Lord of Glory
Lifts the cup to bless the Wine.
We who reenact the Story
Seek the Savior in the Sign.

More than just an illustration
Thought it is but Wine and Bread:
This, the Spirit's proclamation
Of the Holy One who bled.

It is more than just a symbol
Though it is but Bread and Wine,
For the Spirit flows, as nimble
As the sap within the vine.

More than just a silent Letter
Lying dormant on the Page,
This is Truth that breaks its fetters,
Vaults the intervening age.

Words like Transubstantiation?
Too precisian to define
How the Lord takes up His station
In the Bread and in the Wine.

Although we, like doubting Thomas,
Need to see the Hands and Side,
He is gracious with the Promise:
"Come, behold them where they hide."

It is more than just a token,
More than just a word about;
With this Bread, we must be broken,
Like this Wine, our lives poured out.

In that mysterious oblation
Faith is strengthened and restored.
With refocused adoration,
Saints rejoice to meet the Lord.

So again the Lord of Glory
Lifts the Cup to bless the Wine.
We who reenact the Story
See the Savior in the Sign.

The Tryst

Did their eyes meet before he turned away?
Although the Lord had prophesied the gist,
He seemed affected by that final twist.
So much a simple gesture could convey:
A friendship you would think could last the day
Evaporating like the morning mist.
And he was not the first to be so kissed;
The question echoes still, *"Et tu, Brute?"*
So much a simple gesture can convey.

"Surely, This Man Was..."
The Centurion Speaks

"Things are not always what they seem: we drove
The spikes through wrist and ankle bones to bind
The criminals up on the cross. We spliced
Their flesh to wood with iron; thus we strove
To make secure what fates the gods had twined--
And generally that view of things sufficed.

But that last Jew clean put me at a loss
To tell what held up what. Have I gone blind?
No! I would swear that, when he paid the price,
I saw the world suspended by the cross
        From Christ."

Hymn: Spiritual Vision
To the tune of "Amazing Grace"

The gaping sockets blankly stare
    Beneath the bony crown,
Skull-like, always grinning there:
    The Hill outside the town.

A lonely sentinel, it stands
    With shadow grim and chill
Above the landscape it commands:
    The Tree upon the Hill.

The very Sun would hide its face,
    Not strong enough to see
The blight now brought to such a place:
    The Man upon the Tree.

But sunlight never could have showed
    Nor eye of flesh have scanned
The grievous Burden of the Load
    That rested on the Man.

Only weakness could have won,
    Only frailty freed
Us from the Burden laid upon
    The Man upon the Tree.

The Centurion Speaks Again

No question but it was a dirty job.
    The scourging by itself was bad enough;
    To drive the spikes, though, really takes a tough
And calloused character. The women sob,
The victim screams, and even as the mob
    Cries out for more, men wince. The really rough
    Part comes when all four soldiers huff and puff
To raise upright the heavy wooden stob,

For then the man's own weight begins to work:
    The tendons crack, the flesh begins to tear--
    And when he thinks it's more than he can bear,
They drop him in the socket with a jerk.
    And after we did that, he said (it's true!)
    "Forgive them, for they know not what they do."

The Paradox

The irony: the angels came to sing
    To shepherds, while the scribes slept through the night
    Condemned, and incognito came the king.
The Magi came from far away to bring
    Gold, frankincense, and myrrh, and learn by sight
    The irony the angels came to sing.
Herod found no humor in the thing,
    And Joseph woke from sleep to sudden flight,
    Condemned and incognito, from the king.
Mary found it food for pondering,
    And often in her heart she would recite
    The irony the angels came to sing.
But there would be no final reckoning
    Of what it meant, 'til up Golgotha's height,
    Condemned and incognito, came the king.
And now it's left for us by faith to cling
    To him whose empty tomb brought full to light
    The irony the angels came to sing:
Condemned and incognito came the King.

The Chest of Iron

And I dreamed, and behold, in my dream I saw the Cross, and the Lord was on it, and he could hardly breathe for the suffering of his body, its tendons stretched and twisted, the bare bones grating against the spikes as he raised himself to ease his suffocation. And then he sunk as if struck with a blow, and I saw his soul grasping as it were a great weight, as a heavy chest bound with iron. And I saw that the burden was grievous to him, and hurt him more than the pain of his body, for it bowed him down so that he could not see the face of Heaven. And indeed there was that in the chest which Heaven itself would not look on, for there came a great darkness and woeful thunderings as of the end of the world. And thus I saw the wrath of God revealed from Heaven against all wickedness and evil; for the Lord cried out with a loud voice, and so great was the weight of his burden that it tore his soul from his body, and yet he would not release his hold. And he fell with the weight and struck the earth, and it shook mightily and split asunder to give him passage. And the sky grew even darker, as if light itself had been taken out of it, and the body on the Cross was still.

And I looked and saw that the Lord's burden fell through the earth like a plummet, and so exceeding great was the weight thereof that it fell clean out of the world and into the black void of the Abyss whence men do not return. But he would not relax his grip on it until he came to the pit of deepest Hell, where finally the load found its level and came to rest. And there he laid it down, and stood up tall and strong among the dead, and looked into the eyes of Death himself. And it seemed to me that he spoke with a clear voice and said, "Behold! The burden of Sin which delivers all men into your hand has brought hither the Son of Man as well."

Then I saw that Death grinned, and would have licked his lips but that his face was naught but a skull. But the Lord arose and walked away from the iron chest, and at that Death and all the dead cast themselves upon the ground and wailed with terror. And then I looked closer and saw the reason for their distress: for fastened to each of the dead by an iron chain was just such a chest, though smaller, the tremendous weight of which kept them in that place. And the chains were so strong that none but the Ancient of Days himself could break them. Thus was the Son of Man revealed in his glory, and even the dead, who could die no more, dreaded to look upon the face of God.

And the Lord laughed, and aweful was the sound of his joy in that place. And he said, "Did you think that the chest was *mine*? No, but I say to you that in it lies every weight of Sin which afflicts my chosen ones!" And I looked, and behold, at the sound of his laughter a great number of the chains fell in pieces, and the chests they had bound were shattered, and lo! The contents thereof were all found in the great trunk which the Lord had brought. And those souls fell to their knees and worshiped, and were found in that place no more. But great was the horror that remained upon the rest, also a great company, and there was weeping and wailing and gnashing of teeth.

Then I saw that the Lord locked that great chest with strong locks that none could open, and he left it there, and laughed in the face of Death and walked out of his dominion, and took a three days' journey back to where his body awaited him in Jerusalem. And the chest remained in that place, and so great was its weight that neither Death nor Satan himself nor all his hosts could lift it or move it thence. And there it shall remain, though time and the world should end a thousand times, to trouble the saints no more.

Guard Duty

I
Saturday Night

"The elements are simple: flesh, and stone,
     Shroud, seal, silence, watching guard,
     Dew, lingering smell of myrrh and nard;
Deserted by his friends, he lies alone.
A prophet, touted once for David's throne,
     A good man and a healer; but he jarred
     Their consciences just once too often--hard--
And so became a bag of rotting bone.

We've seen a lot of cases: other men--
     Messiahs always end up in a tomb,
     The elements the same. As you'd assume,
Their names are never heard on earth again.
     And this one's won't be either, I dare say."
     It was almost the dawn of the third day.

II
Sunday Morning

"Don't get me wrong. I saw the Romans kill
     The blighter, and they did a thorough job.
     But stones that size just do not roll uphill
     Unhelped, and if his people came to rob
The tomb, I'll eat my hat. O.K., I'll take
     The money and pretend that's what they did.
     But I've just got a feeling it won't make
     The truth--whatever it may be--stay hid.

The whole thing simply makes no sense. If he
    Was really the Messiah, tell me why
    The Romans rule and Israel is not free,
    Or why, for goodness' sake, God let him die?
Yet--when the stone rolled, just before we fled,
    I'd swear I saw him walk out from the dead!"

III
Sunday Evening

"All we had to give was a night's sleep
To keep the prophet's ragtag band of men
From making the whole situation worse
By stealing the corpse. That stupid bunch of sheep?
Their only thought was saving their own skin!
Their shepherd struck, they scattered — more's their
    curse.

So how they pulled it off I'll never know.
They must have snuck in when the earthquake came
And got out quickly — that's the official tale,
And all you'll get from me. I'll tell you though,
You're no one's fool, and so I would not blame
You if you thought it was a little frail.

Come, here's an inn; I'll buy--now, not a peep
Of where I got the money! I'll be in
More trouble than a legion could disperse.
[whispered] It was a fine conspiracy to keep
    His name from ever being heard again
    That put the Temple silver in my purse!"

Firstfruits

Silver that does not tarnish,
Iron that will not rust;
Wood that needs no varnish,
Flesh that is not dust;

Gold that will not perish,
Love that won't grow cold:
Hopes we ever cherish,
Dreams we tightly hold.

For in the human heart
Old stories still survive
Of one who took our part,
And died, --and is alive.

The Will

When our Lord chose the Church to be his bride
        He did not chide,
But took her sins as dowry, though it bled
His life's blood out to bear them, and he died,
Bequeathing his estate. The will was read
And published throughout all his kingdoms wide.
"I here leave all to her whom I have wed:
Forgiveness, life, myself no longer dead,"
        Was what it said.

Resurrection

When Christ was nailed to Calvary's central cross
  And his bright blood flowed out, the sun was pale;
  For in the Son's sunset the sun was lost,
  And thus in mourning, morning's light was veiled;
And thus in darkness shrouded, Phoebus sailed,
  Until in glory bursting from his tomb,
  And having conquered sin and death and hell,
  The rising Son broke, shattered, split the gloom,
And at Son's rising sunlight was resumed.
  And angels sang, for in that light the day
  When sin and death would meet their final doom
  Was set, ordained, as Holy Scriptures say.
And still the light shines forth, though sometimes dim,
  That then was kindled in Jerusalem.

Firstfruits 2

The saints believe what every lover knows
    Who, gazing on one face, can plainly see
    The glory latent in the flesh: a rose.
If Love is what leads lovers to compose
    Their songs of praise and deeds of charity,
    Then saints believe what every lover knows.
The truth the Heavens declare, the Firmament shows,
    To starry-eyed and moon-struck is most free:
    The glory latent. In the flesh, a rose
Can shine in cheeks as brightly and disclose
    To opened eyes as deep a mystery
    Which saints believe and every lover knows.
Yet ash to ash and dust to dust it goes,
    An aching void its only legacy,
    The glory latent in the flesh. A rose
Will lose its petals, yet the Spring bestows
    New life; but what hope for the flesh can be?
    The saints believe what every lover knows:
The Glory latent in the Flesh arose.

Conjunction

At the fulcrum of the Cross
A host of concepts meet:
The Profit hidden in the Loss,
The Victory in Defeat.

The Acceptance, the Rejection;
The Worship and the Jeers;
The Freedom in Election,
The Ecstasy in Tears.

The Mercy and the Justice;
The Human, the Divine;
Pilate; Judas; Jesus--
The broken Bread, the Wine.

The Maker of Orion,
The Victim of the Scam;
The Meekness of the Lion,
The glory of the Lamb.

Pentecost
(Compared with Later Imitations)

Stronger than a hawk, the Dove
Swept by, and in the eddies of
His passing, tongues of flame were fanned
And men fell to the ground unmanned.
They stuttered as their wits were lost
And thought it a new Pentecost:
The merely inarticulate sigh
Of His furious passing by.

But when He stopped to build His nest
First in the Apostolic breast,
A different language was expressed
In fit words, honed and well disposed;
Those were not drunk as men supposed,
But spoke real tongues they had not learned:
Thus the true tongues of fire burned.
Men heard about their sins and grieved;
They heard the Gospel and believed,
For each one heard of Jesus' blood
In his own tongue—and understood.

Does that Dove's nesting in the heart
Drive it and the mind apart?
Never! Rather, say He brings
The two together 'neath His wings.
The mind alert was not the cost
Of the primal Pentecost,
Where true wit was not lost, but gained
When the showers of blessing rained.

Road to Damascus

"I am Jesus whom you persecute."
       "If you're the Christ, why isn't Israel free?"
       I'd thought it something he could not refute.
He did not argue;   he was almost mute,
       His searing radiance just content to be:
       "I am Jesus whom you persecute."
And I was on a journey, resolute
       To stamp his sect out once and finally.
       Death was an answer that they could not refute!
But how they faced it shook me to the root,
       And now this Flame was burning into me,
       "I am Jesus whom you persecute."
Gamaliel had taught me all the fruit
       That reason could produce--a Pharisee,
       I had traditions no one could refute--
But now it was all burning into soot,
       The Fire blinding me so I could see:
       "I Am Jesus whom you persecute."
It was a Reason I could not refute.

The Commendation
(Rom. 5:8)

In all mankind no greater love can be
      Than to lay down
One's life for a good friend. But look around,
      And you will see
A man, to save his spiteful enemy,
      Lie down to die--
      No other reason why.

And does God then commend His love in this?
      While we were yet
Sinners, in our sins still firmly set,
      With Judas' kiss
Still warm on our lips and His cheek, the hiss
      Still ringing, "Crucify!"
      He willingly did die.

And so we hear the glorious decree,
      "Reconciled!"
And I, who would have stood there and reviled,
      Now on my knee
Search in vain for something that could be
      A fit return
      For grace I did not earn.

And I, who solely by His sacrifice
      Now live,
Will never find a single thing to give
      That would suffice
To pay back one ten-millionth of the price
      He freely gave
      To save me from the grave.

Ah, well, I must give all; my grateful heart
      Could do no less.
Yet, in so doing, freely I confess
      There is no part
To give He has not purchased from the start.
      Before His throne,
   I give Him but His own,

And worship Him for grace beyond my art
      To think or tell:
By death and love a double debtor made,
I find all debts in Him forever paid.
      He doeth all things well!

The Lord's Work

In the name of the Father,
For the sake of the Son,
By the aid of the Spirit
All that is worthy is done:

All that's a boon to the Body,
Knitting its sinews in love,
Taking the News to the nations,
Born on the wings of the Dove

For the increase of the Kingdom,
Unto the glory of Grace,
By the means of the Mercy,
Longing to look on the Face.

Apologia

Structured steps within the Dance,
Things which could not be by chance:
Architecture of belief?
Arch of bole and vein of leaf.
Crystal's angles; raindrop's curves;
Bone and sinew knit with nerves.
Flick of wrist, fly-toss, and then,
Break of bubble, flash of fin.
Beyond these sure and certain hints,
A clearer class of evidence:
Broken fever; opened eyes;
Dove descending from the skies.
Footstep firm on slope of wave;
Stone rolled back from Jesus' grave.
Glory growing out of grief?
Architecture of belief;
Things which could not be by chance:
Structured steps within the Dance.

Counting Poem

One Person, two natures; three Persons, one God;
Four Gospels, four portraits, one Person—it's odd.
Five wounds on one body; six days and then one,
Morning and night since the count was begun.
The stars of the sky and the fish of the sea:
Twelve tribes, one People redeemed and set free.
Sixty-six books, forty men, many ages,
But only one message through all of its pages:
One Lord, one Faith, one Baptism, one
Way to the Father in Heaven: the Son.

Destiny
(Commentary, Ephesians 1:3, etc.)

As basic as breath,
As lucid as love,
A lyrical light;
Despoiler of Death,
He derives from the Dove
Celebration of sight.

The grain in the board,
The hand in the glove,
The star in the night:
The saint in the Lord
        Shining bright.

Ascriptions II

The Son's a servant; so's the Lord a king
    Who, when a dragon had usurped his lands
    And led his people captive, down did fling
    The gauntlet, slew the foe with his own hands.
The Lord's a king, but so's the Son a lamb
    Led out to slaughter as a sacrifice.
    See how the bright blood stains his side! One gram
    Were richer far than ten Cathays of spice.
The Son's a lamb, but so's the Lord a lion;
    The Church, the tribe of Judah, is his pride.
    He leads them by still waters there in Zion,
    But their best drink flows from his hands and side.
King, Servant, Lion, Lamb; he who's adored
    By all these names deserves one more: my Lord.

I Peter 1: 24-25

    All flesh is like the meadow grass,
        Her glory as its flower;
    Sun beats, wind blows, the seasons pass;
        They wither in an hour.

    The petals fade and fall and die;
        Their fate, like ours, is sure.
    Not so the Word of God! For aye
        It lives and shall endure

Summation

Great is the mystery of Godliness given
To men, in Man's very flesh manifested:
Deftly the wing of dove descending
On voice from vaulted Heaven riven
Vouched for his virtue, tried and tested;
Many a mighty messenger wending
Far from the hallowed halls of Heaven
Watched the saints from Satan wrested;
Soon the sword, asunder rending
Flesh and spirit, flashed, driven
Into joint and marrow, bested
Unbelief and evil, ending
Devil's darkness. Dare the frame
Of mortal man, albeit mending,
Stand before the fearsome Name
Of Glory given to Him who came?
    He came befriending.

Summation II

Our God reveals himself in persons three;
      His Son incarnate is with natures twain;
      From them comes oneness in diversity
      The which hath Holy Spirit for its name.
The Father is the Center and the Head;
      The Son, begot before all time, the Heir;
      The Spirit doth regenerate the dead
      Because the Son hath loosed them from Death's snare
By being born a man, of humble birth,
      And living a lowly life of servanthood,
      And spilling his pure blood upon the earth
      When Pilate nailed him to the rough, crossed wood.
He died and rose; His Death and Life afford
      New Life to those who bow and call Him Lord.

Coming

By every dead and risen corn of grain,
By every word of prophecy declared,
By every lamb on every altar slain,
By every scapegoat led away and spared,
He came to people who had been prepared.

By all the suffering multitudes he healed,
By all the simple parables he taught,
By lost sheep and the lilies of the field,
By his friendship with Iscariot,
He came to them--and they received him not.

By all the prophets and apostles said,
By every thought that ever has been true,
By every drop of blood the martyrs shed,
By every spring when life begins anew,
He comes to us--and now, what will we do?

Commentary, Revelation 21: 24-27

The marching orders of the Great Commission:
   Disciple every tongue and tribe and nation?
   The Torah-nurtured culture of the Jews
Was not enough. A richer far rendition
   Was needed for the fuller celebration
   Of God's creation and the happy news
That Christ had come to earth to take our part.
   Every language's enunciation,
   The cadences of every culture's muse,
Their architecture, eloquence, and art—
   And nothing, sanctified, would He refuse.

On to Nicaea

" ...fides quaerens intellectum." --Anselm of Canterbury

From the first day the Gospel was proclaimed,
The passionate intellect was there, demanding,
Not proof—the Empty Tomb provided that—
But reasoned explanation that was aimed
At faith in search of fruitful understanding
For mindful worship, not for idle chat.

So the Apostles, sent to meet this need,
Defined with care the doctrine they were handing
To their disciples; they, to those who sat
At their feet. Faithfully they sowed the Seed,
Watered, weeded, wept through heat and cold
(Scripture was the standard, guaranteed,
By which they worked as on the seasons rolled),
Until it brought forth light a hundred-fold,
A wholesome harvest on which yet we feed.
The climax of this process was the Creed.

The Way

At first the Faith was simply called "The Way,"
     The narrow path that leads from death to life;
     Not just a set of rules we must obey,
     But One whose dying was the death of strife.
Not just a guide—the Truth is much more strange.
     To follow Him? I never could begin
     Had He not simply made the Great Exchange
     Of all His righteousness for all my sin.
Yet I do follow Him, for when He died
     I died, and now I live because He lives.
     I walk now in the life His death supplied,
     The Way of lawful Love His living gives.
The Truth: His death was Life. That's why they say
     At first the Faith was simply called "The Way."

Credo

The content, the commitment we express
    When mind and heart embrace the ancient Creed
    Are faith and fealty. That we confess
Our faith means it is more than just a guess:
    Our Lord's own blood is what has guaranteed
    The content, so commitment we express.
Acknowledging the Law that we transgress,
    We find forgiveness, know that we are freed
    To faith and fealty when we confess.
We walk by faith, not sight; still, nonetheless,
    We've tasted and we've seen, and so we feed.
    The content's the commitment we express.
This ceremonial assent, this "Yes!"
    Flows gladly from both mind and heart: the deed
    Is faith and fealty when we confess.
Not just a ritual; it is more, not less:
    We stake our very souls, for when we plead
    This content, the commitment we express
Is faith and fealty when we confess.

The Sign

Fiercely focused, aimed from eternity,
    He set his face like flint toward the Cross.
    Nothing could turn Him back: the Tempter's gloss,
The wrath of Herod, raging of the sea,
Well-meant advice from friends who could not see.
    It wasn't that He failed to count the cost;
    No one knew better how to weigh the loss,
But He maintained His gaze on you and me.

A wicked generation seeks a sign;
    It's different when you're given one instead.
All the meaning centers, every line,
    Himself, His sacrifice, and all He said:
Fiercely focused, still we sip the wine;
    Aimed for eternity, we eat the bread.

The Supper of the Lamb

Hatred is the hunger fed;
Fear can make the mighty pine.
Plaited briars crush the head;
Splinters grate against the spine.
For the ruler and the priest,
The King of kings provides the feast.

Ravenous revenge is sped;
The demons gain their dark design:
Drawn by livid lines of red,
Gnats and flies descend to dine.
For the angel and the beast,
The King of kings provides the feast.

The hands are clenched, the arms are spread,
The knees are twisted out of line;
The blood congeals, the breath is fled,
The body is to dust consigned.
Earth's appetite has never ceased:
The King of kings provides the feast.

The Seed descends into its bed,
Out of sight and out of mind.
The world is turning overhead;
The rain will fall, the sun will shine.
From the grain of corn deceased,
The King of kings provides the feast.

Brought to focus in the bread,
Freely flowing in the wine:
Drawn by living lines they've read,
The sinner-saints ascend to dine.
For the greatest and the least,
The King of kings provides the feast.

Hoc Est Corpus Meum
An Exercise in Grammatico-Historical Exegesis

"This is my body," said the Lord,
    And offered in His hand
The bread He'd picked up from the board.
    What would they understand?

Could there be any doubt of what
    Was body, what was bread?
Of what was body, what was not,
    Of how the words were said?

"This is my blood," the Savior said,
    And handed them the wine
With hands through which it pulsed and sped.
    How would they then assign

Potential meaning to the words
    So fraught with life and doom?
Can we now hear the way they heard
    There in the Upper Room?

Some have a fear they will forsake
    The meaning and the power
If literally they do not take
    The words of that grave hour.

What was done and what was said
    Took simple bread and wine
And made them—into flesh and blood,
    Or into Seal and Sign?

To share the drama of the scene
Back in those days of yore
Is how to fathom what we mean
By this strong metaphor.

Prayer

Father, we pray to thee;
Humbly we say to thee
Words that convey to thee
More than they tell.
Far from the sight of thee,
Blind to the light of thee,
Fearing the might of thee
Here where we dwell,
What can we say to thee?
Humbly we pray to thee,
Teach us the way to thee,
Lost when we fell.

The Disciples' Prayer

Oh Thou whose thoughts are far above my own
As are the stars above this whirling stone
We call the earth; who know'st the thoughts I think
Before I think to think them, though I shrink
To let Thee see them all; whose soul doth burn
With purity, and more, whose heart doth yearn
To see that flame of love also in me--
When I bow down before Thee on my knee,
What words have I that would be fit to say?
He said, "Just Father, Abba Father, pray."

So: that which I could never have begun,
Thou, sending forth thine own beloved Son,
Hast done, accomplished: washed my sins away
So that as thine adopted child, I may
Approach thy throne--yet where shall I begin?
My purest thoughts are tainted yet with sin.
And though thy Spirit stirs my heart to pray,
To such a One as Thee, what shall I say?
Show me my deepest need, my highest aim!
He said, "Begin with 'Hallowed be thy Name.'"

Yes! Reverently to set thy Name apart,
Grant it the highest place in all my heart,
And crown it there because it speaks of Thee,
Thy greatness and thy grace poured out on me;
And so to come into thy courts with praise
And in thy gates my thanksgiving to raise--
Ah, nothing less than this my heart could give:
To crown Thee king of all my life--and live.
And what is next, now that I have begun?
"Just this: 'Thy kingdom come, thy will be done.'"

Oh Thou who rulest in the Heavens above
Where Angels, burning with reflected love,
Flit forth like wings of wind or flames of fire,
Thy will their only thought, their sole desire;
If only I could be thine instrument
On earth as they in Heaven, with pure intent!
Since I believe thy promise to be true,
Do Thou work in me both to will and do
Thy pleasure. What more can I ask? He said,
"Fear not to ask me for your daily bread."

Thou who didst go to Calvary and bleed
To purchase everything that I might need--
What wondrous condescension this, that Thou
Should'st stoop ev'n to concern Thyself with how
I am to be kept, housed, and clothed, and fed!
How sumptuously thine earth produces bread
For sparrows! And Thou causest it to yield
A wardrobe for the lilies of the field.
And yet, how soon thy goodness we forget!
As we our debtors, please forgive our debt.

He said, "I do forgive you every whit
Your sin, for Jesus paid the price for it,
And you have freely bowed to Him as Lord
As evidenced by this, your very word
In asking for forgiveness; further still,
Your wish to pray according to my will
And for my glory." What else should I request?
For Thou alone does know just what is best.
He said, "Into temptation lead us not,
But save us from the Devil's evil plot."

Thus do I pray, and thus shall ever pray:
From thy dear side, Lord, let me never stray.
For I am weak and prone to every sin

Unless Thou cleanse me constantly within.
Oh, sanctify me with thy Truth, lest lies
Of Satan tempt. Teach me to keep my eyes
Fixed ever on thy Word, and thus on Thee.
For Thou alone, and naught that is in me,
Alone thy greatness and thy sovereign Grace
Can save and keep me 'til I see thy face.

For thine it is to rule o'er everything,
Thine alone the kingdom, Thou the king;
Thou art a shield, a rock, a fort, a tower,
Thou burning strength, thine all alone the power;
And every line of thy salvation's story
Shouts Mercy! Grace! and Glory! Glory! Glory!
What Thou hast been, forever Thou wilt be,
And I thy grateful slave on bended knee.
So be it: I, who once loved self and sin,
Delight to have it so; and so, amen.

Commentary, Hebrews 6:6

Behold it, battered beyond recognition:
    It gazes, hardly human, through the thorns.
    Weeping tears of shame, yet still it scorns
To call down angels and abort the mission.
Wonder, then, how long in this condition
    It can endure to be so bruised and torn,
    To bear fresh wounds on those already born
And still remain strung up on exhibition.

The world looks on and thinks it comprehends:
    "Another Promise failed, a Name besmirched;
So must all false Messiahs make amends."
    You recognize, impaled upon its perch,
The Body of our Savior? Oh, my friends—
    This is the other Body of Christ: the Church.

There Then Abide These Three
For Father Ronald Murphy

And what is Faith? Not simply to believe
  Unless Hope is no more than wishful thinking
  Or Love a cynical disguise for lust.
Evidence and reason can relieve
  All valid doubt, and yet still leave us shrinking
  From what we do not love and will not trust.

Reason is necessary, not enough.
  Soul-conquering Love must come alongside, linking
  The mind in Hope to One who felt the thrust
Of all our hate and still looked back in love.
  In *Him* we trust.

Commentary, I Peter 3:15

We are to keep ourselves in readiness
    Should any ask a reason for the hope
    That is within us and which we confess.
The great Deceiver does not sleep or rest,
    Enticing people toward the slippery slope,
    And so we keep ourselves in readiness.
The Truth is lovely in a silken dress;
    Her servant comes in sackcloth tied with rope,
    A humble penitent who must confess
His great unworthiness, but also stress
    Her grace, the only reason he can cope,
    And thus he keeps himself in readiness.
We are but beggars sharing our success
    With other tramps who also want to grope
    Toward the light with us. And we confess
That ours is not the brilliance we express.
    Christ is the Light; we aim the telescope:
    That's how we keep ourselves in readiness
To justify the great Hope we confess.

The Dance

The dance is faith. What must we then believe?
    When God the Son stepped forth, how did it mesh,
    The human, the divine, together weave?
    The saints confess He came, and in the flesh.
He came, and in the flesh, and came to die.
    Was that the only answer He could give?
    To sin it was the only apt reply.
    No lesser step could let His people live.
What is the fruit, what is the evidence
    Of genuine new life that's from above?
    An unforced and robust obedience
    That does not grow from guilt but leaps from love.
It leaps from love, that deep divine Romance,
    The waltz that is the Trine eternal Dance.

The Invitation

Let sound the sackbutts;   come, cornettoes, call
    The folk to feast and joyous revelry.
    Already lute and lyre fill the hall
    With sweetest sounds of merry minstrelsy.
The Lord beneath his royal canopy
    Himself shall sit as host, for he abounds
    In kingly kindliness and courtesy.
    Hold back for no unworthiness! He frowns
On base ingratitude, but loves the sounds
    Of Joy unearned, unearnable, delights
    To honor those who come. The call resounds,
    For one last moment echoes in the heights.
Surely you're coming with us? Do not doubt!
    The door that closes shuts forever out.

Pentecost

For many days the little band had stayed
Together, meeting daily in the room
While time grew heavy with a sense of doom,
And every moment that it was delayed

Seemed an eternity--but they obeyed.
To waver would be rudely to presume;
It seems they'd learned their lesson at the tomb,
So patiently they waited and they prayed.

That morning seemed no different, much the same....
Then unexpectedly there came a sound,
A hurricane of wing beats, tongues of flame
Which blew them out into the streets around

Articulating praises to the Name,
When, swifter than a hawk, the Dove came down.

The Beneficiaries

But few of wealth or power,
Not very many wise
Will in the final hour
Rise up to claim the prize.

So what of those elected
To gaze upon the Face?
Not perfect, but perfected:
The trophies of his Grace.

ಓ Book III ೮
The Tales of Taliessin

By

Donald T. Williams
Professor of English
Toccoa Falls College
Loremaster
King's Poet in Succession
King's Man

Illustrated by

Ruby Dunlap
Professor of Nursing
Belmont University
King's Lady

The Minstrel

Prelude:
Taliessin at Glastonbury

"The starveling hermit praying in this cell
Was once the mighty knight Sir Lancelot.
Pass quietly, but look upon him well.
The path from many-towered Camelot
Has many twists and turns, but to this spot
It leads. Might you have leisure for the tale?
Well, rest we then beneath yon spreading oak."
He sat and twitched aside his hooded cloak,
Resting a small harp upon his knee.
"I was King Arthur's minstrel," then he said,
"My job: to keep the Great Hall filled with glee.
And all those golden days, so quickly fled,
Passed in all their sorrow and their glory
Before my hungry ears and watching eyes.
        And so, if otherwise
You've heard in legend or in allegory
Some version of the deeds that there were done,
Allow one who was party to the story
To speak. No greater honor e'er was won--
Or lost--in any land beneath the sun."
He bowed his head in memory of the king,
        And then began to sing.

Prologue

Darkness lies deep upon the vales of Britain.
    Terror lurks in the forest, flows from the sea;
    The remnants of Roman order fall or flee--
The lucky ones pierced by spear or sword-smitten,
The survivors harried, hiding, hunger-bitten.
    Vain the spell of Druid under tree,
    Vain the power of priest on bended knee,
Vain the blade with ancient runes written--

The merciless heathen roams the land at will.
    In Tintagel, surrounded by the storm,
    Igrayne sits pondering. The hearth is warm.
"That dream I had the night my lord was killed . . .
    Oh--OH!" A sudden chill invades the room;
    Arthur the king is restless in the womb.

The Minstrel

The minstrel struck his golden harp;
The music sounded strong and clear,
Like edges keen and arrows sharp
    In hands of warriors bold.
Like rivers swift and mountains sheer,
Like the North wind blowing cold,
It stirred the very blood to hear
    Him strike his harp of gold.

And then the bard began to sing:
If all alone his melody
Could build so bright and shimmering
    A vision in the heart,
What charms of might and mystery
The spoken spell, the subtle art,
The wisdom and the wizardry
    Of wordcraft could impart!

So deep was the enchantment laid,
So masterful his minstrelsy,
So strong the music that he made,
    The story that he told,
That all the gathered chivalry
Would hearken 'til the night was old,
Entranced and still, whenever he
    Took up his harp of gold.

The King's Mariners

The wind was fair, the ship was yare,
    The crew was skilled and bold.
Exotic wares and spices rare
    Were bursting from the hold.
They gave the slip to pirate ships
    And sailed on seas untold;
The prow did dip, the yards did drip,
    And still the ocean rolled.

The wind doth rise, the captain cries,
    The crew doth furl the sail;
The wind, it dies; the captain sighs,
    The crew grows wan and pale.
And then the wind starts up again;
    The sailors' hearts do quail--
The boards do bend, the thunder dins:
    She rides before the gale.

Six nights and days the sky did blaze,
    The spray did chill the bone;
Through mist and haze, uncharted ways
    The fleeing ship was blown.
Six days and nights the storm afrights,
    The crew doth strain and groan
'Til from the heights the lookout sights
    A shore no man has known.

The Kings Mariners

The seventh day the sun's bright ray
    At long last shines again.
Rejoicing, they behold a bay;
    The helmsman steers them in.
The vessel stops, the anchor drops,
    The harbor they do win.
Their brows they mop 'neath mountain tops
    Where man has never been.

They break their fast, repair the mast,
    The hunstmen go ashore.
The stormy blast through which they passed,
    They think on it no more,
But of the land which lies at hand
    And begs to be explored.
And so they stand upon the sand;
    They hunt the deer and boar.

From west to east they chase the beasts
    Through forests thick with fern.
From great to least, they share the feast;
    They feel their strength return.
And now desire burns like fire
    And every heart doth yearn
To climb up higher, mount the spire,
    Secrets strange to learn.

When they had been a mile or ten
    In silence wandering,
They came within a hidden glen
    And found a wondrous thing.
Upon a green they saw fourteen
    Maids dancing in a ring;
And they had seen the faerie queen,
    And sweetly did she sing.

To ask how long the elven song
      Was heard? No one could tell:
The dancers hung their notes among
      The stars like silver bells.
The mariners hark while skies grow dark,
      The notes, they rise and swell.
And then they mark the morning lark,
      Unbroken still the spell.

Full still they kept, 'til one man stepped
      Out bold to join the ring:
The dancers leapt, the sailors wept;
      It was a grievous thing.
The vision flies, the tune, it dies,
      No more the dancers sing.
The queen, she cries; before their eyes,
      The elves are vanishing.

They tramped around the island's bounds
      To hear that song again,
But no more found that magic sound,
      Too pure for mortal men.
They hoist the sail, they say farewell;
      Thoughts turn to home and kin.
And yet they wail to leave that dale
      They saw the dancers in.

For many a week they hardly speak,
      Each thinks his thoughts alone.
The sky is bleak, the wind doth shriek,
      And chill them to the bone.
But wisdom now sits on each brow;
      They know what they have known!
The helm knows how to turn the prow;
      The vessel sails for home.

The wind was fair, the ship was yare,
    The crew was skilled and bold.
Exotic wares and spices rare
    Were bursting from the hold.
They gave the slip to pirate ships,
    And came from seas untold;
The prow did dip, the yards did drip,
    And still the ocean rolled.

Merlin
Taliessin Telleth of Meeting Him in the Forest

The man who here sits, and moves not, nor speaks,
But watches in wakeful, wide-eyed silence,
A shadowy figure may chance to meet
Who slowly, slowly, slow approaches,
Taking form as it comes.

Falling hair, like a flood of water
On rocks of shoulders, splashes silver;
Eyes like coals that ever smoulder
With eerie fire flash from the shadows,
Growing more bright as they come

Vision
Taliessin Speaks

Think how the Moon, the mad enchantress,
Crowned by the silver of covering cloud,
Rides o'er the shimmering, shivering sea-waves
    No ship's prow has plowed . . .

Think how the sound of singing voices,
Chanting softly, a sigh in the air,
Mingles its notes with the moonlight shining
    On Hesperus' Garden fair . . .

Think of the Moon, and the surf, and sea-magic,
    And they will take you there.

Scene

The rain comes driving, slanting through the mist.
    The trees and sky, a blur of grey and green:
    Impressionistic brush-strokes on the screen
By a Chinese artisan with dancing wrist.
And there, beneath a sheltering tree, the tryst.
    Oblivious to the weather, they are keen
    On what from words and glances one may glean:
She lifts her face up to her knight, is kissed.

The raindrop and the teardrop on the cheek
    Are mingled, flowing in the self-same track.
And are they tears of joy? The sky is bleak.
    It seems their kiss has sealed a solemn pact:
He lifts her to his steed; away they streak;
    They fade into the mist, do not look back.

The Conversation of Taliessin

When one of Arthur's knights desired peace
For thought, he might traverse the colonnaded
Path which left the high hall toward the east,
Then through an arch into a secret, shaded
Garden, where all Nature's bounty, aided
By unobtrusive Art, had made a place
Of richness and of order and of grace.

For there were coverts deep and shadowy,
And there was sunlight warm upon the grass,
And there were fountains bubbling merrily,
And there were pools as smooth and clear as glass.
There one on pathways lined with stones might pass
By flocks of deer that wandered unafraid
Through flowery meadow and enchanted glade.

And though it was not visible to sight,
A subtle patterning of symmetry,
A balance of proportion, never quite
Obvious--a hidden harmony
Of part and whole, a sound felicity
Of shape caused those who wandered there to find
Composure welling up within the mind.

And there at whiles Taliessin would walk,
Sometimes alone, sometimes with two or three
Of noble lords and ladies, and their talk
Would be of beauty and the brevity
Of life, of valor and of sanctity,
Of love; and often on such days their words
Would scale the heavens like a flight of birds.

The Conversation of Taliessin

Sir Balin le Sauvage was not a knight
To dally much with love or courtesy.
His talk was all of puissant deeds in fight,
Of famous sieges, tourneys, strategy,
Of glory won by arms, of victory.
Why he was in the garden on that day
('Twas not his custom), no one there could say.

Taliessin was saying, "We must ever
Keep these things in mind and hold them fast.
For if we should lose them, they may never
Return in our time. And if the past
Foretells the future, then they cannot last."
In disbelief Sir Balin shook his head
And clapped the poet on the back, and said,

"My friend, thou needest purgatives I ween.
Come, be a man and don't make such a fuss.
Why, look around you! Has there ever been
A king so great and knights so glorious?"
The minstrel struck his harp and answered thus:
"Aye, by God's grace they are indeed. But, then,
I am a man, and they are only men."

    "And what is man?"

Balin turned.

"Intricate engine angels might admire,
        Material spirit, animated earth,
        Crafted casket for celestial fire--
        Doomed to die the day it has its birth.
Hands that open, befitting a gracious lord,
        Able to touch a cheek as soft as mist,
        To wield a pen, a brush, a harpsichord--
        But just as apt to freeze into a fist.
Godlike image, able to stand erect,
        Yet by what small and simple things laid low:
        A sneeze, a scratch, a germ, and all is wrecked;
        A few short years, the time has come to go.
Delicate instrument of Love or Lust,
        Admirably compacted--out of dust."

And Balin turned disgustedly away
And clanked off in his armor, but Elayne
And Percivale to Taliessin said, "Pray,
Good Sir, continue." Down a grassy lane
They strolled, extolling in a gentle vein
The Virtues, and their conversation ran
On love and on the mystery of man.

The Philosophy of Taliessin
The Soul

A simple center of focus, a fury of order
>   Which takes from available matter what it needs
>   To body forth itself; a heart that bleeds
Discursive Reason; more, a rapt recorder
Of all that passes, and a subtle sorter
>   Of all that it collects; a fount of deeds;
>   A seedling sown, itself a sower of seeds;
Establisher of I/Thou/It, the border.

Thus God created it; corrupt, it stays
>   The same, though in corruption: chaos creeps
In everywhere; the order all decays.
>   The matter mutinies; the memory sleeps;
The fountain flows polluted; in a daze,
>   The Reason wanders--and the Reaper reaps.

Origin of Language

The Origin of Language
Taliessin Lectureth in the School of the Poets

Then Man, the wielder   of Words, awoke,
Saw the sunlight   slanting down,
Saw the ground-fog   swelling upward,
Heard the light   laughter of leaves,
Climbed the mountains,   mist-enshrouded,
Felt the wind,   wet with rain,
Saw the stabbing   stars in darkness,
Watched the antics of   wild creatures,
Heard within his   head the sounds,
Pulled them forth,   in patterns ordered,
Uttered into   air around him
Liquid Names;   in lilting language,
Spoke the mighty   Spell of Speech.

The Balladeer

The Balladeer

The king unto his troubadour
Said, "Come, a ditty while we sup:
Some sample of your ancient lore
To lift the weary spirits up.
Some tale of hero true and brave
Who faced the dragon's fire alone
A damsel or a town to save
And got for his reward a throne.
A lay of beauty and of dread,
Of starlit sky and distant shore,
A ballad of enchantment," said
The king unto his troubadour.

The minstrel took his lyre up,
His fingers poised upon the strings;
And motionless stood knife and cup
To watch the melody take wings.
So silence reigned throughout the hall,
And then the troubadour began
With notes like drops of rain that fall
Upon a parched and burning land.
First soft, then like a torrent down
It flowed, and swept them all away,
Beyond the walls, beyond the town
Beneath the waning light of day.
They heard the western sky turn red,
Then fade away to black. They heard
The stars glint silver overhead
Until the morning breezes stirred

A land where they had never been.
A lull came, and they drained the cup.
'Twas e're such like enchantment when
The minstrel took his lyre up.

He stood; the words began to flow.
With them the sun rose bright and clear,
And then the knights beheld the foe--
And hand was clenched on hilt for fear.
They saw the green and glittering scales;
They heard the rumbling of his blaze;
They felt their hearts begin to quail
Beneath the venom in his gaze.
They felt the dragon's baleful breath,
Surveyed the worm's appalling length,
And knew why men could long for death
Rather than assay his strength.
They saw the ruined countryside,
They saw smoke rising in the sky,
They saw the serpent's ramping stride,
And then the worm began to fly.
Then darkness came upon them all;
They flung them down to wait for woe,
Save one bold warrior, strong and tall,
Who stood; his words began to flow.

"Come Death, Destruction, Flame, and Fire,
Come Malice, Madness, evil Spell,
Come Darkness, Doom, or Dragon's Ire,
I still defy thee, Fiend of Hell!"
He took the flame upon his shield;
It melted fast onto his hand.
The sword his other arm did wield
Became a beaming fire-brand.
What no mere mortal blade could do,

Heat from the worm's own evil heart
With one sword wielded fierce and true
Did: tore the gleaming scales apart.
The blood spurt scalding from his side;
The dragon roared and rose in pain;
A hundred tons of ravaged pride
Fell in a ruinating rain
Upon one still undaunted knight
Who scorned to raise his useless shield,
But lifted up with all his might
The sword, and thus his fate was sealed.
Down came the worm, the knight went down,
But drove his point into its heart.
Then came a blast and dinning sound
To split the very sky apart.
A searing blaze leapt in the air;
The worm was his own funeral pyre.
But also on that warrior fair
Came death, destruction, flame, and fire.

The tear flowed freely down the cheek
Of comrades in that bitter glade;
They cursed their hearts, too slow, too weak
To stand and give their brother aid.
But then the flames began to part,
And, striding forth, the hero came:
For those who pierce the dragon's heart
Become impervious to flame!
Then down as one upon the knee
They fell, and took him as their king.
He swore them there to fealty
Upon his sword, still glistening.
So courage rose within each heart,
And with their oaths they gave it breath:
Ne'er more from duty to depart
Come fire, flame, destruction, death.

"They kept those vows in many deeds,
But those come in another tale;
And now, my brothers, we must needs
Drink our lord's health in frothy ale."
Thus ended the good balladeer,
And none could find a word to speak:
The last note faded in the ear;
The tear flowed freely down the cheek.

It seemed no time had passed at all;
It seemed eternity had run.
But as they left the banquet hall,
They saw the last light of the sun.
The night passed o'er them peacefully,
The day saw many a noble deed.
They gathered once more, gracefully,
For meat and drink and golden mead.
The king received them royally
And greeted warmly one and all.
Since last they'd bowed the grateful knee,
It seemed no time had passed at all.

The king then to his troubadour
Said, "Come, a ditty while we sup:
Some sample of your ancient lore
To lift the weary spirits up.
Some tale of hero true and brave
Who faced the dragon's fire alone
A damsel or a town to save,
And got for his reward a throne.
A lay of beauty and of dread,
Of starlit sky and distant shore,
A ballad of enchantment," said
The king unto his troubadour.

Some Real Magic
Taliessin Lectureth in the School of the Poets

Within the cadences of human speech
    Attentive listeners can sometimes hear
    The rhythm of the wave upon the beach
    Or listen to the music of the spheres.
Within the small sphere of the human eye
    The watcher who knows how to look can see
    A spirit that's as lofty as the sky
    Or humble as the lover on his knee.
When in the alembic of the human mind
    Imagination boils with memory,
    Such vision with such sound can be combined,
    Far more mysterious than alchemy!
The Philosopher's Stone we vainly sought of old
    Could never have made such rare and costly gold.

The King's Chapel
Taliessin Remembereth
the Time of his First Entering Therein

The marble columns grew like trees;
They arched above your head to soar
In light and branching traceries.
Between the boles, the forest floor
Was touched by shafts of colored light
Which slanted through the middle air
From windows high exalted there
Past motes of silver dancing in the height
Like thoughts with wings that wheel from trees in flight.

It was a world of air and stone
Indwelt by silence, light, and thought,
One pilgrim wandering in alone,
And sound of breath in wonder caught.
In such an arbor, how could I
But guess at what the gardener meant?
His arches reaching seemed to hint:
For so much weight of stone to soar so high
Was like a marriage between Earth and Sky.

True Love
Eric in the Wooing of Enide

"Thou art the truest Treasure of my heart,
A Lantern in the darkness shining bright,
Unerring Inspiration of my art,
All this," unto his lady said the knight.

"Thou art the Friend who understands the Dream,
The Hand on cheek or shoulder laid so light,
The perfect Comrade to complete the Team,
All this," unto his lady said the knight.

"Thou art the Choice impossible, yet willed,
The Vision unforeseen to bless the sight,
Desire unfulfillable, fulfilled,
All this," unto his lady said the knight.

"And I, the poorest knight in all the land,
Unworthy of such grace or such delight--
Yet I will serve thee!" As he kissed her hand,
All this unto his lady said the knight.

Air
A Song of Taliessin

While walking out under the greenwood fair
    A maiden I chanced to meet
Who softly whistled a country air,
    And the melody was sweet:
As sweet as the blossoms she twined in her hair
    Or the grass 'neath her dancing feet;
She softly whistled a country air
    And the melody was sweet.

I hid me back of the cedarn bough,
    The better that tune to hear:
It smoothed the furrows from off the brow
    And filled the heart with cheer.
Like the lonely seaman who peers from the prow
    With his home port drawing near,
It smoothed the furrows from off the brow
    And filled the heart with cheer.

Never again did I see the maid;
    The tune I cannot recall.
But every melody that's played
    And pleases me at all
Sends me back to that greenwood fair
    And seems to echo the beat
Of a softly whistled country air
    Whose melody was sweet;
    The melody was sweet.

The King's Mariners, II

The captain laid the sextant on the table;
The first mate laid his finger on the chart.
A hundred weathered seaman, strong and able,
Felt a sudden chill about the heart.

"Strike the mainsail; drop the anchor; batten
Down the hatches!" cried the mate with dread:
For "*Terra Incognita*" read the Latin,
And "There be dragons here!" the English said.

Then up upon the deck the knight came striding,
Covered, cap-a-pie, with shining mail.
Far North and West the vessel had been riding
Across the waves, hot on the monster's trail.

Ultima Thule they had left far behind them.
Their world was roaring ice, fantastic lights,
And eerie whalesong, serving to remind them
How great his peril who the dragon fights.

Yet memories sustain them: children screaming,
Farms and villages awash in flame.
And so the valiant knight in armor gleaming
They've brought: St. George of England is his name.

The lookout scans the sky for signs of trouble;
Into the longboat then the warrior climbs.
The sea against the ice-floes foams and bubbles;
The sailors think upon the dragon's crimes.

Four hardy seamen are the knight's companions;
The captain puts the lance into his hands.
The worm lies hidden in the frozen canyons;
"Lower away!" the bo'sun then commands.

The sea is restless, and the spray is chilling;
The knight is soon deposited on shore.
One thing is sure: a dragon he'll be killing,
Or warmth of hearth and home he'll know no more.

The crevasses are turning and they're twisting;
'Round any bend the deadly foe might lie.
The sky is sleeting heavily and misting.
Soon either St. George or the worm must die.

The crevasses are twisting and they're turning;
His boots upon the ice refuse to grip.
The mist turns foul; the ice seems to be burning.
He readies the lance and prays he will not slip.

Amidst the reeking fumes he fights confusion.
It will not do to charge here; let the worm,
Angered at the warrior's rash intrusion,
Pounce here where no footing can be firm!

Even amidst the stench that he was making,
The dragon caught the hated human smell.
Aroused to wrath, and caution all forsaking,
He launched himself, full hideous and fell.

Never before had any been so daring;
Never before had any been so bold,
Across the frozen ocean to come faring
And taunt the evil serpent in his hold.

Around the bend he came with nostrils burning;
But at his heat the ice began to melt.
His sharpened claws were flailing and were
        churning;
Helpless, he slid toward where the warrior knelt.

Focused, calm, the knight continued kneeling.
His prayer done, he knows he has one chance:
The legs push upward, now! The blow he's dealing;
Into the dragon's mouth he drives his lance.

Stunned by the blow, the knight falls backward,
        sprawling
Across the slippery ice, but keeps his grip.
The lance snaps, but the dragon too is falling;
The scalding life-blood foams about his lip.

The crevasse was collapsing, melting, steaming.
How he got out, the warrior never knew.
Back on the ship, he thought he had been dreaming,
But blood-caked mail and blistered skin showed true.

Songs of praise were sung that night at matins
As swiftly South, toward home, the vessel fled.
For "*Terra Incognita*" read the Latin,
And "There be dragons here!" the English said.

Cliges to Phenice

Beloved, gaze in thine own cloistered heart.
    A secret Garden has been planted there
Of Nature's growth refined by subtle Art
    Where nothing thrives but what is sweet and fair.

And yet the sweetest and most wondrous places
    Are buried deep. Thick hedges and high walls
Protect them from the coarse, intruding faces,
    Far from the mocking laughter that appalls.

Yet once a lonely knight came wandering there,
    Let in by some mysterious Grace, to roam
The most secluded paths. And in its air,
    He breathed the long forgotten scent of Home.

So, Lady, seek in thine own cloistered heart
    The secret Garden thou hast tended. There
Now dwells the Knight who lives to take thy part,
    Who never more will leave that land most fair.

Taliessin Playeth Chess

A pawn moves out to open up a lane
    Which might allow a bishop to advance.
    Three moves ahead--at least--anticipate!
Beware the lurking knight. He lurks in vain;
    The square he wants is covered. With a
        glance,
    We spot potential weakness. So, we wait.

If we can bring just one more piece to bear,
    The trap is ready. So proceeds the dance.
    If not perceived until it is too late,
This seemingly inconsequential square . . .
    "Checkmate!"

Elementary
Taliessin Lectureth in the School of the Poets
*"And the world was without form and void, and darkness was upon
the face of the deep. And the Spirit of God was brooding upon the
surface of the waters"* (Gen. 1:2)

Earth, Water, Wind, Fire
Each against the others strain
Until the stronger God, Desire,
Binds them in the Golden Chain.

Water, Wind, Fire, and Earth
Mix in Chaos uncontrolled
Until sweet Order, brought to birth,
Links them in the Chain of Gold.

Wind, Fire, Earth, and Water,
Each of which, in Nature's course,
Would make the world's foundations totter,
Bow before a greater Force.

Fire, Earth, Water, Wind
Perform what they've no knowledge of:
Find their unity and end
Within the Golden Chain of Love.

Harmony in universe;
From cacophony, a Choir;
Thus does Grace redeem the curse
Of Earth, Water, Wind, and Fire.

Lancelot and Guinnevere

Lancelot and Guinnevere

A laugh, a word, a careless fling,
An innocent desire to please:
That such a little thing could bring
A kingdom to its knees!

The subtle sign, the clicking dice;
A failure to perceive the clue:
Such a small thing will suffice
A kingdom to undo.

A lingering look, a heart that aches,
A dainty eyebrow arching, coy:
Such a tiny thing it takes
A kingdom to destroy.

A brother's trust, a failing nerve,
A knowing smile, a jealous frown:
Such a paltry thing could serve
To bring a kingdom down.

The knight his lady must obey;
An interview behind the wall:
Such petty things, to be the way
To make a kingdom fall.

A deadly game of blindman's bluff--
A stroking hand, a tilting chin:
Such minute things, to be enough
To do a kingdom in!

The True History of the Holy Graal

As it was handed down faithfully from father
to son in the household of the King's Poet mentioned herein,
and thus preserved; which true account was made known unto
Sir Thomas Mallory, Knight: but he most wickedly and blame-
fully did suppress the same for the inordinate love he bore
to the French Book; and which is now written down
by Donald the Scribe, as he heard it from
the mouth of the last descendant
of Taliessin the King's Poet
of Camelot; and
he asks that the
reader hereof
may pray
for his soul's health.
Amen.

The knight on the barbican buckled his baldric and strode
Down by the stairway steep 'til he stood in the gate.
Far in the distance, the dust he had seen in the road
Grew imperceptibly solid. Simply to wait
Was his task as his eyes slowly focused a figure of fate.
A single horseman emerged at the head of the cloud,
But no sun shone like lightning from byrnie or plate:
No gallant knight was he to dazzle the crowd,
But he came to counsel the king, as he before had vowed.

No coat-armoure he wore, nor needed none;
    Of simple woolen cloth he wove his weed,
    And that with purfling nor vair. A cloak of dun
    Sufficed to clothe him. What more might he need?
    No caparison covered his sturdy steed,
    Nor crupper, for no saddle would he wear.
    His master held no reins, but told his beads;
    His hood thrown back revealed his tonsured hair,
For shepherding Christ's flock was all his earthly care.

He slid from his horse before the castle door,
    And laughed, "What ho, sir Knight! We meet again."
    "And never a day too soon. Our need is sore
    Last Logres fall through foul excess of sin.
    The king fears the presumption of our men,
    Who drop their duty to pursue the Graal
    Through holt and health, through mountain, plain, and
        fen,
    While robbers multiply and widows wail--
Yet how can aught so holy tell and evil tale?"

With such plain words the knight addressed his guest,
    Who crossed himself in fear and thus replied:
    "The fault lies not within that chalice blest,
    But with the men who follow it through pride,
    By which same fault our father Adam died.
    For look you: holy also was the fruit,
    And holy the command that he defied;
    So in wrong arrogation was the root
Of harm that followed. Thus, that error I refute."

"That is well said," the knight replied, "and yet
    It does not answer to our present need."
    He summoned a servant as he spoke to let
    The parson's horse into its stall to feed,

While through the courtyard he his friend did lead.
    The sound of tabour, cithern, lute, and lyre
    Came filtering through the air. "I see indeed,"
     Replied the priest, "The question is a mire.
For who can tell the Called from those who just aspire?"

"That cannot I," said Kay the Seneschal.
    "The king sits brooding o'er the empty Table,
    And bids you come unto him there with all
    The speed that you can muster. If you're able,
    As soon as you have rested, we'll"--"The fable
    Of that great board has gone through all the lands,"
    The preacher interrupted, "and that table
    Is empty now?" "Nearly so it stands.
The quest of the Sangraal has sorely tied our hands."

The parson slammed his hand against his fist
    So sharply that it made the courtyard ring.
    His eyes grew stern, and through clenched teeth he hissed,
    "I will not rest, nor wash, nor eat a thing,
    Nor do aught else until I've seen the king."
    The knight turned up a stately marble stair,
    Then through a colonnaded porch to bring
    His guest to where the cinnamon-scented air
Wafted through the chamber Arthur found most fair.

It was the fairest room in Camelot,
    If not indeed in all of Christendom:
    Perfectly round and windowless, yet not
    One hint of darkness there could ever come,
    For Merlin's magic chased away the glum
    Tartarian shades. Two spherical, crystal jars
    Ever silently circled 'round the room,
    Glowing with the light from two most knightly stars;
One with white of Venus, one with red of Mars

It was the fairest room in Camelot.

In any spot their lights by turn would blend,
       Or one have dominance while the other waned.
       So traveled they, and never found an end--
       An endless circle all their course contained.
       And so their pleasing influence they rained
       Upon the arras rich which hung the wall,
       Whereon was woven by hands both skilled and trained
       The seasons blending, winter unto fall,
And wondrous deeds of knights who sat in that great hall.

There was the king himself when, as a squire,
       He'd pulled the sword clean whistling from the stone
       And stood amazed as multitudes cried, "Sire!"
       Then some years later when his strength had grown
       And knights begun to gather 'round his throne,
       He was portrayed on top of Badon Hill
       The day the Saxon might was overthrown
       And bright Excalibur had drunk his fill
Of heathen blood, which for the peace he there did spill.

And there was Gawain, wandering in the cold
       Whenas he kept his tryst with the Green Knight.
       Three times his host went hunting. Thrice, all told,
       The guest was baited in a harder fight
       To keep his courtesy and yet do right.
       But though he played right well, he could not win,
       But fell, and had to bide the cruel bite
       Of Bercilak's broad axe. It nicked his skin,
Which otherwise through faith unbroken might have been,

And all because he would not bluntly turn
      Aside the proffer sweet of fin amoure
      From his fair host's good wife, who feigned to burn
      With lust to see if Gawain would abhor
      Adultery or Venus' courtly lore.
      For courtesy forbade him to refuse
      Whate'er his lady asked, and Christ, who bore
      His sins, would not allow him so to lose
His chastity. The knight was caught, and could not chose

Between the two fidelities, nor know
      What course to take, and so he did accept
      The magic, life-preserving garter; so,
      Halfway between the two extremes he stepped,
      Revealing not his winnings; thus he kept
      Not faith entirely with either lord.
      Full sorely for that cowardice he wept
      And bitterly repented, and implored
Forgiveness, and for sin his very life abhorred.

He gathered the green girdle 'round his side
      In token of his trespass, and took leave
      Of Bercilak, nor longer would abide,
      But homeward took his way. His heart would heave
      At each thought of his failure. No reprieve
      Seemed possible. He stood before the board
      Of Arthur, and did there this doom receive:
      Each knight would wear the girdle with his sword
In token that Sir Gawain was to grace restored.

And there was Lancelot the time he went
      To rescue Guinnevere from Maleagant's hand,
      And in her service was not discontent
      To ride in the disgraceful cart, to stand
      The coward's part two days in tourney, and
      To cross the sword-bridge on his hands and knees;

For all which he received her reprimand
    Because for two short steps his heart did freeze
Before he climbed into the cart, the queen to please.

Full many a tyrant's neck was pictured there
    Beneath the foot of one of Arthur's knights,
    And many a castle, town, or damsel fair
    Which had been rescued from its woeful plights
    By those brave warriors in their valiant fights.
    There also many a baleful dragon's doom
    Was chronicled beneath the glowing lights
    Which ever silently circled 'round the room,
Shining on knighthood pictured in its fairest bloom.

And in the center sat the Table Round,
    About which stood one hundred twenty seats.
    A greater wonder nowhere could be found,
    Nor ever center of such knightly feats,
    For here the heart of Arthur's kingdom beats.
    Yet now it beats but weakly. Can the hard
    End be upon us, deepest of defeats?
    Modred and Taliessin the bard
Alone remain of all that with the king have warred,

And Kay the Seneschal, and now the priest.
    "Hail, Sire!" said the latter as he bowed,
    "Lo, I, who of your servants am the least,
    Have heard your call and come as I have vowed."
    The king's voice sounded weary, but still proud:
    "Well met, Sir Priest! Arise and hither come,
    And tell us if Providence may have allowed
    Some means this deep morass of mire to plumb,
And save the fairest fellowship in Christendom."

The parson noticed that Taliessin
    Looked up with courteous eyes to hear his speech,

- 234 -

But Modred scowled and turned away. A friend,
He took note, and a foe, then, one of each,
Both sat beside the king in easy reach.
But now he must give thought to what he'll say.
The king had need of wisdom, and to teach
An answer would be hard. No knightly play,
But the Sangraal itself had lured the knights away.

So, "Good my Lord," the cleric then began,
"I would hear more about this grievous woe.
Why did you not these expeditions ban,
Nor e'er permit them from your doors to go?"
The king replied, "I do not fully know.
I would not hold them here against their wills,
And though it may be folly, I was slow
To clean forbid them. One heart maybe thrills
To a true call of God which leads it o'er the hills,

And this to hinder would be grievous sin."
Modred then looked up disdainfully.
"So you see what a cleft stick we are in.
Such reasoning is nonsense, plain to see.
I would have locked them up and kept the key."
"And done us no more good that way at all,"
The bard said, and the king said, "I agree.
The greater part should not have left this hall,
But I am merely man, and cannot sift God's call."

"Sir Galahad the Good is gone away,"
The king continued then, "to seek the Graal.
Tristram the Trusty left but yesterday
With Bedivere the Bold, a bootless bale.
Courteous Gawain's laughing grace doth fail
The court when we have most need mirth to take.
Percival, Bors--I won't complete the tale,

But more than all the knights who me forsake,
I grieve the loss of fair Sir Lancelot du Lake."

"And so do I," the parson shook his head.
        "But although I am priest to God most high
        And sometime chaplain to this kingdom's dread
        And sovereign king, there is no way that I
        Can solve this riddle, for I will not lie.
        I too am but a man, and cannot see
        Beyond what Scripture teaches. My
        Advice, such as it is, can only be
To trust in God, for with the king's words I agree."

And Modred scowled, but Arthur's face was flint.
        "Yet nonetheless, tomorrow I will preach
        In chapel and dispense the sacrament,
        And try by prayer if that I can reach
        Through God the hearts of these good knights, and teach
        Some of them better where their duty lies.
        The Holy Ghost is far the better leach,
        And he can change the heart, to his surprise,
Of any erring knight, to Tarshish though he flies."

"So be it," said the king, "and let us keep
        Our vigil in the oratory there
        This night, and neither eat nor drink nor sleep,
        But on the altar offer all our care
        Up with the parson's sermon and his prayer."
        "This were well done," the priest said, "and let all
        The people of the court who will repair
        Unto the chapel when the sun's red ball
Doth wane, and we as one will on the Father call."

The first bright stars were gathering in the sky
        As Arthur and his courtiers took their way
        Towards the king's stone church that stood nearby

To keep their vigil and to watch and pray.
But some there were whose hearts led them astray:
For Modred's darkened mind could only take
Thought of how the king he might betray,
And Guinnevere, who thought her heart would break,
Prayed not, but only sighed for Lancelot du Lake.

All through the silent night they silent stayed,
E'en Kay, whose knees grew stiff, for he was old.
And some in truth, all in appearance, prayed
And stirred not, though the air grew damp and cold.
And so, while Arthur's errant servants bold
Followed wandering phantoms through the land,
And dreamed of grasping what they could not hold,
And slept but could not rest, some of the band
In Camelot found peace they did not understand.

Come hither, Children, and be fed.

Then prayers grew visible as ghostly breath
        And night was at its darkest, cold and still,
        When, unexpectedly as sudden death,
        There came a sound of chanting that did thrill
        The blood with woeful horror and made chill
        The spirit as the air had done the flesh.
        And all did shake with fear, for every will
        Was laid bare, and then probed again afresh
By an unearthly light which secrets out could thresh.

For it shone from the altar purest white,
        But where it touched a man it was blood red;
        And there stood one in priestly garments dight
        Who held a cup and freshly broken bread.
        "I Joseph am of Arimathie," he said,
        "And henceforth will no more on earth be seen
        Of men. Come hither, children, and be fed,
        For you have need of strength. The times are lean,
And none of you is healthy, nor is any clean."

"All those who seek the Sangraal will return
        Well chastened and repentant of their sin.
        But coals of fire smolder here, and burn,
        That will destroy your kingdom from within
        Unless to true repentance you can win.
        Beware, Oh King! 'Tis not in your own heart,
        But lies as near to you as doth your skin.
        Beware! Your right hand bears a venomed dart
With which your left a death-blow may to you impart!"

Lancelot and Gwynnevere

"Yet since there are those here who have kept troth
 With both their earthly and their heavenly king,
 Nor flitted after fires like a moth,
 But counted their true calling as the thing
 That most pleased God, these tidings I do bring:
 You are the last of living men to see
 The Holy Graal of which the sages sing.
 And so, now do not fear, but come to me,
And let us sup with Him who died upon the Tree."

The fear of some then melted into joy,
 And they arose and took the sacrament.
 But some there were whose hearts felt sore annoyed
 At Joseph's words, and they could not repent,
 But gnawed themselves in rage or lust, and went
 From blackness into blackness, and were drawn
 Yet deeper into sin, nor would relent.
 And then a rooster crowed, and it was dawn,
And when they all looked up, the Holy Graal was gone.

They stumbled forth into the morning light
 And for a moment, found no voice for speech,
 Until the king said, "We have seen this night
 A sight for which we never thought to reach!
 Yet what can Joseph e'er have meant to teach
 With his words of right and left? I cannot bring
 Myself the honor of any here t' impeach."
 But Guinnevere would not look upon the king,
And Modred said, "I swear I did not see a thing!"

They parted then and took their separate ways,
 And wandered long that morning, deep in thought.
 But when the sun had burned away the haze,
 Sir Kay grew lonely and for the chaplain sought,
 And found him with the bard. The three said naught,
 But each from other solace there did take,

'Til the priest sighed, "Ah what joy and pain we've
    bought!
This one prayer for the kingdom I will make:
Let one knight not return--Sir Lancelot du Lake!"

Lancelot and Guinnevere: How It Ought to Have Been
(Taliessin Indulgeth in Wishful Thinking)

Two minds and hearts amazingly akin:
    Begot by Chastity upon Desire,
    They burned with both divine and earthly fire.
Matured already e'er it could begin,
It seemed their love had simply always been.
    But it had not. They found themselves with prior
    Loyalties that asked to be held higher,
But loved each other as they hated sin.

Nothing could turn their fire into ice;
    Their sacred vows they'd not consent to break.
"I will not rate thee at a lower price,"
    He said, "Nor thee nor virtue will forsake,
And this must be my costly sacrifice."
    There really was no other choice to make.

...Modred sneered...

Consequences

Silently the secret lovers crept,
    Trying to believe they left no trail,
    While ever Modred sneered and Arthur slept.
And rumors grew, and Modred was adept
    At sounding true while plotting to rebel,
    And silently the secret lovers crept.
Each tryst, they swore, the last that would be kept:
    And thus they swore and fell and swore and fell,
    While ever Modred sneered and Arthur slept.
Though Guinnevere in private sighed and wept
    And Lancelot was lord of inner hell,
    Still silently the secret lovers crept.
So closer to the precipice they stepped,
    And tottered on the edge, but could not tell,
    And ever Modred sneered and Arthur slept.
And so, headlong, the awful hours leapt
    Toward death, the convent, and the hermit's cell
    As silently the secret lovers crept
And ever Modred sneered and Arthur slept.

Taliessin Pondereth the Past

It was not the heathen pirates that annoyed us.
    Our own propensity to play the fool,
    Our inability to resist, destroyed us,
    Caught in a self-willed trap of dire misrule.
Then Arthur came and took the stone-kept sword
    And wielded it with such nobility
    The flower of knighthood took him as their lord,
    And with their help he taught us chivalry.

We couldn't keep the lesson, and it closed,
    That door through which we briefly glimpsed the Good.
    So Pelles bleeds through lack of a question posed,
    The realm through lack of an answer understood.
A greater King must bring the time when we
    May learn in bowing truly to be free!

Postlude:
Taliessin Reminisces

I was a Singer from my youth
    In silence wandering;
I was a Seeker after Truth
    On nothing pondering.
A student of the stars whose eyes
    Were chained unto the earth;
An heir predestined to the Prize
    Who could not come to birth.

A golden harp upon my back
    On which no string was strung;
A scroll unwritten in my pack,
    No music on my tongue:
Accoutered thus, through barren lands
    I sought I knew not what--
'Til, following unheard commands,
    I came to Camelot.

What was it that you saw in me?
    It couldn't have been much:
A minstrel with no melody,
    A harp no one could touch.
But I knew what I saw in you;
    And all the passing years
Have only proved the vision true
    Which first I glimpsed through tears.

What did I find in you, my King?
The song that I was born to sing!
    And all the passing years
Have only proved the vision true
    Which stung me first to tears.

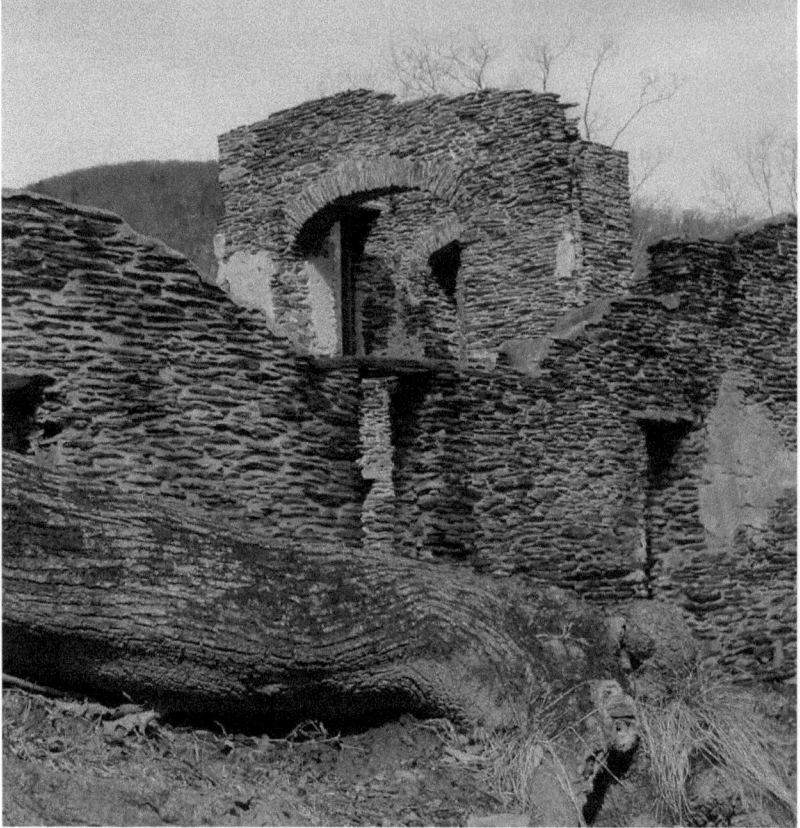

St. John Episcopal Church,
Harpers Ferry, West Virginia

℘ Book IV ℘

**A Labyrinth of Lymericks
And a Clerestory of Clerihews**

A Collection of Light Verse

The Higher Criticism
Limerick #1

A high-critical biblical scholar
Wrote books that all caused quite a holler:
    He claimed that St. Paul
    Wrote *The Campaigns of Gaul,*
And made about three million dollars.

The Muse

You cannot force the sovereign Muse
To lend her aid to grace your views,
For if you try, she will refuse;
And your foul fate (It cannot miss)
Will be to write a poem like *this*!

The Coming of Spring

I ask myself a question 'round this time
Each year, though now first setting it to rhyme.
It is a burning, nagging question: "Is
Spring worth the swelling in my sinuses?"
And though I have my doubts, I must confess,
When all is said and done, I answer, " ...No way!"

On the Philosopher After Death

Riding high on the Life Force's tallest, triumphant wave,
Precariously poised above its lowest trough —
When first he saw things *thus*, his face turned grave,
And Bergson shuddered, and coughed a nervous cough.

Grading

The student's paper, reeking red
　　With ink, looked rather gory,
Littered with the carcass of
　　Another stillborn story.

Another, of the Same

The student's paper, reeking red
　　With ink, looked rather messy,
Littered with the carcass of
　　Another stillborn essay.

Library

A million books and thrice that many cards
Interdependently interlocked and filed:
Physicists, philosophers, and bards,
Some readable by none, some by a child —
And if one thing's misplaced, a frantic, wild
Search is precipitated. Chaos grins;
The staff fights back, but never completely wins.

Art Pour L'art: Limerick #2

There was once a young writer of verse
Whose lines grew increasingly worse.
　　He read them aloud
　　To a violent crowd
And was carried away in a hearse.

Graduate Study: Limerick #3

There was once a great student of lore
Who would sit still and study for more
　　Than a day at a grind.
　　He went out of his mind
And collapsed on the library floor.

The End of Learning: Limerick #4

While writing a long dissertation,
A man made a sound observation:
　　"Once I have the degree,
　　All this rubbish, with glee,
I will burn in a great conflagration."

Inspiration: Limerick #5

There was once a young limerick writer
Whose income grew tighter and tighter.
　　"If I want to make bread
　　With my verses," he said,
"I will just have to be even snider."

The Undergraduate: Limerick #6

There once was a student of grammar
Who was an incurable crammar.
    He studied his best
    On the eve of the test
By beating it in with a hammar.

The Prosodist: Limerick #7

A writer of verse from Hong Kong
Got all of his limericks wrong.
    They started out fine
    From the very first line,
But the last one was always, inevitably, invariably, and without
fail, too long.

Educational Reform: Limerick #8

The colleges of education
Thought up may a grand innovation.
    But once their reform
    Had become the norm,
Not a kid learned to read in the nation.

The Pursuit of Knowledge: Limerick #9

When asked, "Why the ants in your pants?"
The scientist stands up and rants,
    "All the money I make,
    I just have to take
And spend writing away for new grants."

Decadence: Limerick #10

In order to sell his new fictions,
He threw off all social restrictions.
      But his efforts were blocked
      When no one was shocked:
They no longer had any convictions.

The Seven Deadlies Revisited

Behold Mankind, the noble creature,
Like a god in every feature:
No sooner born than he begins
To seek the Seven Deadly Sins
(And others too, without a label,
He does as soon as he is able).
First comes PRIDE, the subtle foe
Which first begins this tale of woe.
Before the baby leaves his crib
Or even learns to wear a bib,
He makes his parents stoop and bow
And serve his every whim right now!
Bring the bottle or the breast;
Do not take out time for rest.
Rock him 'til he falls asleep
Or a vigil he will keep.
If ever they fall in arrears,
He'll avenge himself with tears.
He knows himself to be no worse
Than Center of the Universe,
Until his elders finally
Remember that they and not he
Are in control (for they are bigger).
This knowledge causes them to snigger,

And then a Schedule to enforce.
The baby yells until he's hoarse,
But only thus he learns to live
Somewhere between Take and Give.
ENVY next we have to mention,
For it is Pride's first invention
When it has to deal with things
That time inevitably brings.
When the family's escalated,
Things become more complicated:
Siblings come into his life
With new occasions for strife.
Whatever toy his sib desires,
To that one he himself aspires,
And that alone. No other one
Will do, could possibly be fun.
(That is, of course, until his brother
Decides himself to want another.)
'Til Envying what another hath
Inevitably leads to WRATH.
The toy not yielded, in despite,
There now proceeds a screaming fight,
That certain high-pitched, piercing whine
Which means, "You give that back--it's mine!"
A sound that every parent learns
To recognize. When Envy burns,
It gives off flames of Wrath, and this
Also: the smoke of AVARICE.
Never let your children see
The toy commercials on TV.
The more it costs, the more they'll cry
That that's the one you have to buy
(Also the easier it breaks
And more assemblage that it takes)
'Cause everybody else has one,
And he alone never has any fun.

(Of course the toy box is already
Fuller than the wallet of J. Paul Ghetty
With good toys that they never use.)
So only let them watch the News!
Now, ever since old Adam's curse,
Things have gone from bad to worse.
Continue to observe this child,
Like a lamb so meek and mild:
During meals he seems a monk;
There is no place in all his trunk
For veggies or for casserole.
Starve the body, feed the soul!
Until the pious hermit sees
The Golden Arches through the trees.
French fries and potato chips
Slip so easily past his lips;
Candy, cakes, and pies withal
(As long as not one mineral
Or protein or a vitamin
Ever is allowed within).
Such is the sin of GLUTTONY
In a skinny tot of three.
Well, ever since old Adam's curse,
Things have gone from bad to worse.
Show me a Mom who has not said,
"Get in there and make your bed!
Pick your clothes up off the floor
So someone can get through the door!"
Now, he can run ten miles a day,
Lift weights, ride bikes, and swim, and play
At football. But go cut the grass?
You don't know what it is you ask!
To any such thing he is loathe:
He has learned the sin of SLOTH.
But e'er we reach the worst despair,
There shimmers in the chilling air

Perhaps the slightest sigh of hope:
"Maybe yet I still can cope.
So far, only six I see--
From one at least he will be free!"
Well, I don't like to see you frown,
But I will have to let you down:
Ever since old Adam's curse,
Things have gone from bad to worse.
His body is not made of wood;
He'd be LECHEROUS if he could!
Let him grow a few more years;
He will justify your fears,
And you will long for days of yore
With merely tantrums on the floor
To trouble your tranquility.
And if you ask, "How can this be?"
If you ask me, in a fit,
"Why then do we put up with it?"
My answer is a question too:
"Why does God put up with *you*?"

Ars Praedicandi: Limerick #11

There once was a prominent pastor
Who was a proficient bombaster.
      He ranted so loud
      That the bulk of his crowd
Had to come with their ears stuffed with plaster.

Neo-Orthodoxy: Limerick #12

That great theologian, Karl Barth,
Wrote with deep philosophical art.
      He thought that the Word
      Was both God's and absurd,
For his mind was half Paul and half Sartre.

From Antioch, with Love: Limerick #13

Though the lions were starved and rapacious,
That just made his faith more audacious.
      He traveled to Rome
      Like a child coming home
To his Father's voice calling, "Ignatius!"

Leviathan: Clerihew #1

Thomas Hobbes
Was frightened of mobs.
He thought life apart from the court
Was nasty, poor, brutish, and short.

Scholasticism: Limerick #14

When superfluous thoughts troubled Ockham
Like tails wagging dogs just to mock him,
      He whipped out his razor,
      As sharp as a laser,
And calmly proceeded to dock 'em.

Tractatus: Clerihew #2

Wittgenstein
Was known to opine,
"Whereof we cannot speak,
We ought to shut our beak."

Indubitably: Limericks #15-18

There once was a man named DesCartes
Who asked, "Where should Philosophy start?"
    He said, "If I can doubt it,
    I'll just do without it.
Now, that ought to make me look smart!"

So he doubted the clear and the plain
To see what would finally remain.
    'Twas thus he found out
    There was no way to doubt
The doubt in the doubter's own brain.

"I exist!" then with joy he concluded.
"On this point I cannot be deluded:
    Even though it sounds dumb,
    If I think--*ergo sum*!"
To this day he has not been refuted.

If you ask what this tale is about,
It's that doubting must always run out.
    For you never can doubt
    That you're doubting the doubt
That you doubt when you're doubting your doubt.

Walden II/Beyond Freedom and Dignity
Limerick #19

A psychologist named B. F. Skinner
Said that man was conditioned a sinner.
  He proved it with stats
  He collected from rats
Who were there just to get the free dinner.

Bentley: Clerihew #3

Edmund C. Bentley
Was called, evidently,
By Clio the Muse
To invent clerihews.

(He did not refuse.)

An Enquiry Concerning Human Understanding
Clerihew #4

David Hume
Would never presume
To credit a miracle;
He was much too empirical.

Some Sketches from the History of Modern Philosophy
Limericks #20-25

If a tree in the forest falls down
When no one with ears is around,
　　　　Though it crashes like thunder,
　　　　Philosophers wonder
Whether there's really a sound.

Or else, when you exit a room,
Is it logical then to presume
　　　　That the Table or Chair
　　　　That you left is still there
Until your sensations resume?

Bishop Berkeley set briskly about
Proving beyond any doubt
　　　　That the Table and Chair
　　　　Were really still there:
God still saw them when you had gone out!

Dr. Johnson kicked stones and said, "Thus
I refute this ridiculous fuss!
　　　　They may think I'm dense,
　　　　But I've got Common Sense."
He was surely an ornery cuss.

Do you think we have learned any more
Than our ancestors knew back before?
　　　　Now the Chair and the Table
　　　　Are only a fable;
The Room has a lock on the door.

Deconstruction has buried the key
In the depths of the Post-Modern sea.
    So we all stand around
    Or we sit on the ground,
And we call it the freedom to be.

The Interpretation of Dreams: Clerihew #5

Sigmund Freud
Grew very annoyed
When his superego tried to slam the lid
Down on his id.

Homily: Limerick #31

There once was a homiletician
Who was bad about vain repetition.
    Though he chose a new text,
    His people were vexed
When the points were the same old edition.

The PreSocratics: Limericks #26-30

Men once thought that it would be nice
To step in the same river twice.
      But then Heraclitus
      As if just to spite us
Said, "No! Once will have to suffice."

"The water is flowing away;
The new that arrives does not stay.
      Therefore, my conclusion:
      All else is illusion.
There is Change; that is all we can say."

Parmenides answered, "Not so!
The stream doth eternally flow.
      What is permanent's real;
      So, whatever you feel,
There's no motion and no place to go."

He went on, "Heraclitus, you dunce,
Why attempt such ridiculous stunts?
      With no motion or change,
      You can't even arrange
To step in the first river once."

Is the world all in flux or immutable?
The answers both seemed irrefutable.
      But while they were debating,
      Some children went wading,
Once--twice--and it seemed somewhat suitable.

Picard's Perennially Perfect Potable

Some people swear by coffee
As loud as loud can be;
But for the truly civilized,
A cup of Earl Grey tea.

Some long for port or cognac,
White wine or vin rosé;
But far more elegant than these:
A small sip of Earl Grey.

Some swear by Coke or Pepsi,
The Uncola or RC;
But those who really want the best
Request some Earl Grey tea.

And some must have their Perrier;
Some could have had V-8.
But those whose taste is most refined
All think Early Grey is great.

The captain of the Enterprise,
He sails a starry sea;
He asks the Replicator for
A cup of Earl Grey tea.

The captain of the Enterprise,
When first he rises up,
He wants the status of the ship
And Earl Grey in his cup.

The captain of the Enterprise
Will always end his day
With a page or two of Shakespeare
And a cup of hot Earl Grey.

The captain of the Enterprise,
He drinks it by the pot.
Unto the Replicator,
He says, "Tea—Earl Grey—hot!"

While too much Saurian Brandy
Or too much Romulan Ale
Can give you trouble, you can drink
Your Earl Grey by the pail.

Yes, some folks swear by coffee
As loud as loud can be.
But for the truly civilized:
A cup of Earl Grey tea.

The Slide Toward Solipsism Begins: Limerick #32

"Our knowledge," one sage used to rant,
"Is inevitably always aslant.
    The true *Ding an sich*
    Is so sly and so slick
That when you try to see it, you Kan't."

The Consistent Inconsistency of the Old Nature
Makes Self-Reformation Futile
Limerick #33

Before he was saved, St. Augustine
Was in love with the pleasures of lustin'.
  He prayed, "Make me pure,
  But not yet, to be sure!"
While he prayed, his own prayer he was bustin'.

Purgatory
Or, Visiting a Rare Book Shop with little Money

"Do not open!" reads the warning
On the annotated glass.
Leather covers, gold adorning
Kept by polished wood and glass.
"Do not touch. Request assistance":
Just admiring from a distance
Fortifies my sales resistance.
Virgil, with a mild insistence
Whispers, "Look and pass."

All Wet: Limerick #34

"I never," protested Stan Fish,
"Said that readers can make what they wish
  Of a text. The community
  Has that impunity."
Slippery animals, fish.

Across the Pond

"Whilst" instead of "while";
For "Excuse me," "Sorry!"
That's the British style:
A "truck" becomes a "lorry."
What we call a "conservative"
In England is a "Tory."

Americans "drop by"
While Brits "pop over to."
No one knows just why.
A "bathroom" is a "loo."
Americans have to "stand in line,"
While Englishmen just "queue."

We have a "can" for "trash";
They have a "bin" for "dust."
We're "knocked out" when we're bashed;
The English get "concussed."
They stay to leftward when they drive
To keep us all nonplussed.

Two nations thus divided
By a common tongue —
The rule by which we're guided,
However far we're flung:
One of those things the gods decided
When the world was young.

Natura Interdum Vacuum Conservat
Or
Ex Nihil, Nihil Fit
Limerick #35

When using the method Socratic,
One shouldn't be too enigmatic:
  You cannot get blood
  From a turnip or spud
Or by stirring the dust in the attic.

Predestination: Limerick #36

When writing a long dissertation,
On the doctrine of predestination,
  The theologue froze,
  For the words that he chose
Were predestined to cause hibernation.

Homiletics 102: For C. I. Scofield
Limerick #37

The preacher was always enlargin'
On points where no angel would barge in.
  The whole inspiration
  For these bold orations
Was notes that he found in the margin.

Nobody Expects...: Clerihew #6

The Grand Inquisitor
Was seldom a welcome visitor.
His penchant for barbecued sinner
Could be rather awkward at dinner.

The Fundamentalist Creed: Limerick #38

Knowing that sharp deprivation
Is the most assured path to salvation,
Though it gives me great pain,
I vow to abstain
From all pleasures save argumentation.

Argumentation: Limerick #39

To say that his logic was loose
In the texts that he chose to adduce
Would be far too kind;
What came out of his mind
Was closer to audience abuse.

Altar Call: Limerick #40

Such weeping and wailing and curses!
What horrible fates or reverses
Could cause such a thing?
"With our heads bowed, let's sing,
Softly now, one more time, all the verses.

Literature: A Satire

It seems that some shy intellectual Brit
(Most likely a snob and most surely a twit)
    Gets hit
    By a fit
    Of maniacal wit
That causes his neurons to splutter and split.
Well, once this gets started, he just cannot quit
    'Til out he does spit
A story that has at least one naughty bit.
And when this mad fit
    Has finally flit,
    He finds he has writ,
    And that's how we get
The very great bulk of our classical lit
Which exists so that critics can critic their crit
    And so Christians can grit
    Their teeth as they sit
In bold and peremptory judgment on it
    And condemn every whit,
Seeing no reason why they should admit
    That so to conclude
    Without reading a word
    Would be horribly rude,
    Not to mention absurd,
For they already know that it comes from the pit!

Lines on Postmodernism

Modernity's paternity
Produces Post-Modernity,
Where Power is the only good
That can by man be understood.
So Truth is just a sly digression
To serve the interests of Oppression
And anything that sounds sermonic
Just deconstructs to the ironic,
False oppressive rabbit trails
From Dead White European Males.
Extra syllables are the bargain
That we get by using jargon.
Extra meaning? Don't be square!
There wasn't ever any there.
Jargon! Would you like a sample?
Consider this one, for example:
We don't "write books" (the old construction);
Now we call it "text production,"
Where, doubling syllables, we add
The sly hint that the old is bad.
Words of beauty, verse that rhymes,
Are not suited to the times.
Rhythm and alliteration
Are a vile abomination.
Like the plague, all now do flee
Metaphor and Simile.
Detect an Author in the Text?
You'll want to find a Meaning next!
If any 'twixt the lines is tucked,
Poof! We make it deconstruct.
We abhor the putrid scent
Of old Authorial Intent.

In our hermeneutic blender,
Everything's reduced to Gender:
Illustrations of the sin
Of Dead White European Men.
If the work makes any sense,
It only proves the author's dense
And is a vain and snobbish prig.
For Meaning, then, give not a fig!
Only an archaizing fool
Would break this, our most basic rule.
No, let him not ask us to read
Aught with meanings there to heed.
Fractured prose, thoughts torn asunder,
Fill the reader's heart with wonder
And leave her with no grounds to tell
The path to Heaven from that to Hell;
And sets us free to fill the nation
With any old Interpretation,
Immune from being proven wrong
Or right. And thus the Muses' song
Becomes (it's our firm resolution)
An instrument of prostitution
Designed to keep us (aren't we clever?)
In our tenured jobs forever!

On the Quarter Hour: Limerick #41

It certainly is an illusion
That reliably leads to confusion
  When, three or four times,
  Like clockwork that chimes,
The preacher intones, "In conclusion . . ."

Prooftexts: Limerick #42

Though his argument hardly was terse
And was bolstered by verse after verse,
The more that he quoted,
The audience noted,
The more his defense sounded worse.

Frustration: Limerick #43

If slumber is what you pursue,
There's really not much you can do
For your poor nodding head
When you're far from your bed,
And sitting upright in a pew.

Xanthippe: Clerihew #7

Xanthippe
Could be somewhat snippy.
Her husband, Socrates, knew
Her as rather a shrew.

Yahoos: Clerihew #8

Jonathan Swift,
When sufficiently miffed
With the whole human race,
Could put it in its place.

Alliteration: Limerick #44

Mad method of much ostentation,
Sweet sounding sermonic sensation:
  To madden the Muse
  And boldly abuse
The apt art of alliteration.

Altar Call 2: Limerick #45

After one has come down for salvation,
Baptism, and Rededication,
  What's then left to do
  But stare at your shoe
While growth suffers sad suffocation?

Virtue

Wisdom, Justice, Fortitude
Make one rather seem a prude;
All things done in moderation
Sends one into hibernation;
Faith and Hope and Charity
Are certainly a rarity.
Were it not that vice can hurt you,
It would feel much more like virtue,
And too much zeal can sure suffice
To make a virtue seem a vice.
Since goodness then is but a rumor,
Best we keep our sense of humor.

Flowery: Limerick #46

When the eloquence waxes ornate,
It's something the auditors hate.
      The whole congregation
      Just goes on vacation
And dreams of the roast on the plate.

Tradition: Limerick #47

New ideas arouse great suspicion
Lest they clash with unwritten Tradition.
      "It's the way we have done it
      Since Time was begun; it
Just needs, then, your humble submission."

Temperature: Limerick #48

What is the worst theological spat
In ecclesiological tit for tat?
      Could it be inspiration
      Or predestination?
No, worse: adjusting the thermostat!

Carpet: Limerick #49

With faces as smug as the mug of a thug,
With sounds like the snarling of pit bull or pug,
      We pursue the to-do
      O'er the shade of the hue
That the Board recommends for replacing the rug.

Amen: Limerick #50

When the preacher's particular spin
Zeroes in on the horrible sin
    That's afflicting another,
    We shout, "Preach it, brother!
Hear, hear! Preach it, brother! Amen!"

Credo

The saints who once would burn and bleed
Rather than deny the Creed
Now pay no heed to what they say,
Though still they say it anyway.

Confessional: Limerick #51

When trying to make our confession,
We should surely avoid the impression
    (Which would be somewhat rude)
    Of a mere interlude
Before getting on with regression.

In Black and White

What's that on the zebra's back,
Black on white or white on black?
Conundrum to befuddle sight:
White on black or black on white?
Was the contrast then so stark
When Noah shooed them on the Ark?
Had they still such perplexing skin
When he let them off again?
Did Shem and Japheth hold debate
When the stormy nights got late
Over what the proper term is
For their divided epidermis?
Since we still cannot decide
How best to analyze their hide,
Let us leave them to the scholars
Who wear the black/white, backwards collars!

Eschatology: Limerick #52

Though it's something that Scripture berates,
Still it keeps coming out of our pates:
  We can't seem to resist,
  Much less cease or desist
The incessant resetting of dates.

The Sawdust Trail: Limericks #53-55

If your sin's too much drinking of ale,
If it be too much thinking at Yale;
    Whatever you've done,
    The atonement's begun
At the end of the old Sawdust Trail.

If all of your virtue is frail
But all of your vices are hale,
    Get up out of your seat!
    Come down front; let us meet
At the end of the old Sawdust Trail.

If you're caught in the old Devil's spell
And your feet feel as slow as the snail,
    Just lift up your eyes!
    For Heaven's the prize
At the end of the old Sawdust Trail.

A Conundrum: Limerick #56

In pursuit of refined erudition,
We shell out big bucks for tuition.
But where it all goes,
There is no one who knows,
Though the Faculty have their suspicions.

Dordt: Limerick #57

When, deep in our doctrinal fort,
Our stockpile of prooftexts runs short,
When we're feeling surrounded,
By heretics hounded,
We fire the Canons of Dordt!

Anti-Intellectualism: (Including Limerick #58)

The Thought Police will inspect you all,
Interrogate and dissect you all
Lest the horrible plague should infect you all
Which has threatened e'er now to have wrecked you all.
If it has, they will surely detect you all
And pursue you until they have decked you all.
Your excuses will prove ineffectual
And the members will rightly reject you all
For trying to be intellectual.
Though I really can't say I have checked you all,
With all of these rhymes, I expect you all
To be duly impressed
By my passing the test
And not using Lord Byron's "hen pecked, you all."

Jacques Derrida: Clerihew #9

Derrida
Is Post-Modernism's pa.
He thinks that any wisdom which from the
        Ancients we have plucked
Ought to be made to deconstruct.

Pascals's Wager: Limerick #59

There is a Pascal, name of Blaise,
Who has a great game that he plays:
      "I'll make you a wager:
      Now, which bet is sager?
God is; or He ain't; which one pays?"

Limericks: Limerick #60

The list of words rhyming with limerick
Is little, it's short, and it's slimerick.
      But if you can't find it,
      Your readers won't mind it
As long as you give them a glimmerick.

Light Verse: Limerick #61

When writing a verse that is light,
One should always avoid being trite.
      When you dish out advice,
      If you take it, that's nice.
Have I always done so? Not quite.

Economy Class: Limerick #62

A good definition of pain
Is the agony, suffering, and strain
    You inflict on your knee
    When you force it to be
Between two coach seats on a plane.

Spin

What form of madness or inebriation
Comes with the mantle of Administration
To send the conscience into hibernation
    And make the oral cavity
    Descend into depravity
With no defense against prevarication?

Donne: Clerihew #10

John Donne
Twice made a pun
Upon his own name.
Neither was lame.

The Boke of the Courtier: Clerihew #11

Castiglione
Is thought to be phony
By those who cannot appreciate the bravura
Of sprezzatura.

Mary: Clerihew #12

Mary Stolzenbach
Could not be holden back.
On her way to the sky,
She said, "Goodbye."

Frodo: Clerihew #13

Frodo Baggins'
Tail was draggin'.
His trip to Mordor
Was not in a four-door.

Radagast: Clerihew #14

Radagast the Brown
Did not live in town.
Most of his words
Were for the birds.

Diana: Cerihew #15

Diana Pavlac Glyer
Made Humphrey Carpenter a liar.
She showed that, when it came to their influence,
The Inklings weren't truants.

Medical Report: Clerihew #16

Bill Ferney
Went out on a gurney.
One of Sam's throws
Had encountered his nose.

The Fall of Numenor: Clerihew #17

Ar Pharazon the golden
Was due quite a scoldin'.
His trip into the West
Was not exactly for the best.

The Uses of Gesture in Paedagogy: Clerihew #18

Severus Snape
Wears a black cape.
He flicks it with graceful motions
Whenever he lectures on potions.

Marshwiggilian Apologetics: Clerihew #19

Puddleglum
Was anything but dumb.
He put his foot down when the Green Witch
Made her pitch.

The Mary Stolzenbach Memorial Semi-Annual Clerihew Contest of the Mythopoeic Society: Clerihew #20

Mike Foster
Maintains a roster:
The very best clerihewists
In the Society of Williams, Tolkien, and Lewis.

A Note on the History of the Theatrical Arts in the Mythopoeic Society: Clerihew #21

The Not Ready for Mythcon Players'
Scripts were not written by Dorothy Sayers.
But they will always show what mythic feats
Can be performed with borrowed sheets.

Golfimbul: Clerihew #22

Golfimbul:
His brain would hardly fill a thimble.
Who would have ever thought or said,
"He'll be remembered for his head"?

Spontaneous: Limerick #62

A limerick on demand
Has not had a chance to be planned.
        You wrinkle your brow
        Until suddenly, Pow!
It leaps from the pen in your hand.

The Seven Deadlies, part Deux: Limerick #63

There was once a young woman named Lyn
Who foreswore unoriginal sin.
> Though she searched for a new one,
> She never could do one,
So she did the old Seven again.

The Ring: Clerihew #23

> The One Ring
> Was a rather peculiar sort of bling.
> Instead of loudly shouting, "I am here!"
> It made the wearer disappear.

Aragorn: Clerihew #24

> Aragorn
> Was of Arwen long forlorn.
> But then when they were finally wed,
> Before she knew it, he was dead.

Smaug: Clerihew #25

> Smaug the Magnificent
> Was meaner than Maleficent.
> He had a soft spot in his breast
> That let the Dwarves achieve their quest.

Theoden: Clerihew #26

Theoden son of Thengel
Composed a rousing jingle.
He was a grand orc-beater
In Alliterative Meter.

Ioreth: Clerihew #27

Ioreth of Gondor
On ancient lore would ponder.
She had no Athelas, but she could say
"Sweet Galenas" all the livelong day.

Conversation: Clerihew #28

Addison's Walk
Heard some rather splendid talk
The night when Hugo, Ron, and Jack
Tore down the wall 'twixt Myth and Fact.

Research: Clerihew #29

In the Bod
Are parchments rare and volumes odd.
The staff will bring them if you slog
Through their confusing catalog.

Dance: Clerihew #30

The Springle-Ring
Is a merry thing.
You should dance it on the table
Every time that you are able.

Shippey: Clerihew #31

Tom Shippey
Could get rather snippy
With those who thought James Joyce should be
The author of the century.

Daylight Savings Time Ends, March, 2018

Twice a year we have to find the knack
Of springing forward or of falling back.
The time is out of joint; we cannot keep
The daily rhythm of our nightly sleep.
We need the extra hour (Do the math!)
To keep the Sun from setting on our wrath
At being jerked awake while in the dark.
Since Noah let the critters off the ark,
The Seasons managed, without help from us,
To change throughout the year without a fuss.
But now, without an act of Congress, they
(Forget the year!) can't tell the time of day.

The Answer: Clerihew #32

Forty-Two:
That number had a lost to do!
The full account it had to bring
Of life, the universe, and everything.

Shadowfax: Clerihew #33

Shadowfax
Could sure make tracks!
He definitely was a steed
Who could show a chap the meaning of speed.

Wight: Clerihew #34

A Barrow-Wight
Could give a person quite a fright.
But if you can survive, his horde
Might yield a pretty decent sword.

Van Gogh: Clerihew #35

Vincent Van Gogh
Pronounced his name to rhyme with cough.
He gave us all the gift of sight
One brilliant, dark, and starry night.

Tennyson: Clerihew # 36

Alfred, Lord Tennyson,
Dined on pheasant and venison.
'Twas thus he got inspired to sing
About the Idylls of the King.

The Creation of Middle-Earth: Clerihew # 37

Tolkien the young
Made up a tongue.
Then, the better to tweak it,
He made a Folk to speak it.

Peter Jackson's "Hobbit": Clerihew # 38

Legolas Thranduillion
Slew of orcs about a zillion.
Tauriel was there assisting,
Despite the fact of not existing.

The Great: Clerihew # 39

Alfred the king
Commanded his men to make some bling.
He left to us the English throne
Along with a rather impressive Stone.

౭౦ Book V ౪౬

Stars Through the Clouds

Star and Leaf

A newborn leaf and an ancient, lofty star
    Converge in space and time before my eye,
    The one as near as is the other far,
    And both are wondrous things—but both will die.
The leaf will wither in the summer sun
    Or else be blasted by chill winter air
    And wither just the same—it all is one—
    But while it lives, it lives, and it is fair.
Before man woke to see this star was bright,
    And when the last man sleeps it will remain;
    But someday there will be a starless night,
    And nothing, ever again, will be the same.
And yet we pray to One who outlives all
    And know that He will hear us when we call.

We know that He will hear us when we call
    Because of who He is and what He is:
    Creator, Master, Savior, Lord of all
    Whose laughter is the thunder; dew, His kiss.
He feeds his children with a varied feast
    That He grows from soil and sun and summer rain.
    His Word shines out like lightning from the east
    And flashes to the west and back again.
And hark! The piercing clarion trumpet's cry
    That cuts the still night air, unbearably sweet:
    It is the signal of His passing by,
    Some lowly, maybe mortal man to meet.
And at His Name the planets, Venus, Mars,
    Bow in joyful silence, with the stars.

The planets bow in silence, and the stars—
  With one exception: Earth, the haughty, proud
  Kingdom of Lucifer, shackled with iron bars,
  Who neither Joy nor Love nor Peace allows
To pass the warlike borders of his realm.
  He fails! For he cannot keep out the dew
  Nor still the thunder nor the wind in elm
  Nor blot out the lightning. Not a few
Slaves' hearts' bonds have been shattered, charged with
  light
  As bright as noonday sun, and made to live
  A new life by this mystic lightning's strike:
  Redemption sure it offers; life it gives.
This Wonder we proclaim as Lord of all,
  And He it is who answers when we call.

The Goal of the Trivium
Commentary, Proverbs 9:1-6

Old mysteries await fresh revelation.
  Such ideas ought of right to be presented
  In royal garments, rich and ornamented,
Befitting their high lineage and station.
Heraldic manuscript illumination
  In Celtic knotwork swirled and brightly tinted
  For metaphors and the meanings they have hinted:
The setting beckons us, an invitation.

What now seems quaint and esoteric lore
  Was once the simple bedrock of our thought:
  First principles and their elucidation.
That's partly what the wondrous words were for—
  Despite our darkness, they can still be caught:
  Faint echoes of the ancient Conversation.

Some Real Magic

Within the cadences of human speech
    Attentive listeners can sometimes hear
    The rhythm of the wave upon the beach
    Or contemplate the music of the spheres.
Within the small sphere of the human eye
    The watcher who knows how to look can see
    A spirit that's as lofty as the sky
    Or humble as the lover on his knee.
When in the alembic of the human mind
    Imagination boils with memory,
    Such vision with such sound can be combined,
    Far more mysterious than alchemy!
The Philosopher's Stone we vainly sought of old
    Could never have made such bright and costly gold.

Faithful

The harsh will of the gods was the end of Troy;
    Most of the Greeks would never make it back.
    The ones who did found Clytemnestra, coy
    With ten years brooding vengeance to exact,
Or, like Odysseus, were blown off track
    To spend an extra decade wandering.
    But he kept his integrity intact:
    Calypso could not stay his voyaging;
Tied to the mast, he heard the Siren sing,
    But still sailed on toward Penelope.
    Lotus, Circe, Cyclops could not bring
    Despair, could not erase the memory
Which, after twenty years, still drove him on,
    Relentless as the rosy-fingered Dawn.

The "Hex" in the Greek Hexameter

Whom the gods would destroy, they place in his path an
    Occasion
Of lust, fell wrath, or greed, or strong overpowering hubris,
And then they sit back and watch as human nature takes over.
The law of guests is weak, overcome by the lust of the Trojan.
Helped by the cruelest god, the lovely and lithe Aphrodite,
Paris corrupts the heart of host Menelaus' fair consort.
Now the lust for vengeance burns in the breasts of the Argives;
The foul smoke of that fire darkens the eyes of Reason;
The wine-dark sea is stained by the blood of Iphigeneia:
For the life of an infamous whore, they bargain the death of a
    virgin,
And the fleet of a thousand ships sets sail toward the horizon
Of History, or is it Legend? Somehow the distinction escapes
    us.
So Hector's blood soaks the earth on the plains of the breakers of
    horses;
Priam abases himself at the feet of his foe Akhilleus;
The Towers of Ilium crash into irretrievable ruin;
Aeneas, weeping, turns away from the land of his fathers,
Hefts to his shoulders the great and insupportable burden,
Never lives to see the new-found home of the Trojans.
The sons of the Trojan victims travel the path of the conqueror;
Swiftly the Roman Republic degenerates into Empire;
New Hectors spill their blood in futile defense of their
    homelands.
The circle flows to completion, the round shield of Akhilleus,
Only to flow again through the cities of peace and of conflict,
Endlessly turning around, the inescapable cycle,
As Zeus lays down the law: to find the truth we must suffer.

Atrophy

We seem incapable of concentration;
    More than a moment, we cannot be stirred.
    Not all our gigabytes of information
    Can keep the simplest thought from being blurred.
The ancient writers used no punctuation;
    No space was used to set off word from word.
    Still, they preserved for future generations
    The chance to hear the cadence Homer heard.
But now, with electronic inundation,
    Is thought enhanced, or is it just deferred?
    We feed upon our own sophistication,
    And indigestion leaves us undeterred.
Have we the vision yet, the wide-eyed awe
    To see what Homer in his blindness saw?

The Socratic Method

"And so we go our separate ways," he said,
    "You to live and I to die, and who
    Knows which is better?" Taking the long view,
Would waking with that verdict on your head,
Only to take it with you back to bed,
    That you had killed a man because he knew
    That he was ignorant, and said it, too,
Beat having an honored place among the dead?

"Surely they do not kill men there for asking
    Questions," mused the hopeful Socrates.
    But can the dead be killed for any cause?
So did he simply end his life by basking
    In his famous ignorance, or squeeze
    In one more Question laying bare our flaws?

Reflections from Plato's Cave

The fleeting shadows flow across the wall;
      That's all we know. We think they may arise
      Outside our minds, and bring before our eyes
Some glimpse of Truth--but by the time they fall
To us, a faint and hieroglyphic scrawl
      Is all that's left. We try to analyze,
      Deduce from patterns what the shapes disguise--
They're hard to catch and harder to recall.

We think reflections of Reality
      Are cast by Sunlight shining--how we crave
      To turn and look--but still we strive in vain.
No merely mortal man will ever see
      Whether the Door behind us in the Cave
      Is there, so firmly Fate has bound our chain.

So many years we strove against the chain
      That gradually some gave up, and hope was dead.
      "There is no Door; there is no Cave," they said,
"No explanation, nothing to explain.
It's just a game you play inside your brain:
      All the poetry you've ever read
      Makes chemical reactions in your head;
That's all that Pleasure is, and also Pain."

What of the Beautiful, the True, the Good?
      "They're all illusions; they are all the same,
      Sounds upon the wind, an empty name,
And that is all that can be understood."
      But then the rule that says that nothing's true
      Must be applied to their denial too!

So hope could not completely be denied.
     Yet still the shadows flicker on the wall,
     And we're not certain what they mean at all
In spite of every theory we have tried.
If only one of us could get outside
     Into the Light that fills that vaster hall
     And not go blind, but come back and recall
For us the land where the True Shapes abide!

If only--but the ancient Grecian knew
     No way that it could be. It seemed absurd
     To hope or to despair. So still the True
Was but in shadows seen, in echoes heard--
     Until the birth of a barbaric Jew
     Who was in the Beginning; was the Word.

Then and Now

Ambrose read, but never moved his lips.
     Augustine hardly could believe his eyes!
     Where were the sounds that each shaped letter cries?
From page to eyes to brain, and with no slips:
The extra step saved let the saint eclipse
     His peers; the knowledge he could realize,
     Transformed to wisdom by his prayers and sighs,
Caught one who only came for clever quips.

Processing speed has jumped up yet again.
     What are we doing with it? One might ask.
You have to understand the game to win.
     We work, but do we comprehend the task?
A world of pixels, neither voice nor skin,
     And who can find the face beneath the mask?

The Hellene and the Hebrew
Commentary, Rom. 12:1 (KJV)

So where does Athens meet Jerusalem?
    Tertullian couldn't find a single place
    And thus condemned the blind and groping race
To groping blindness. Greeks? Well, as for them,
They asked the Questions brilliantly, but slim
    Or none the odds that they would ever trace
    The Answers, which the Jew in every case
Possessed; the Questions never occurred to him.

Separate, they both remain opaque,
    A price we pay for our ancestral treason.
    The unexamined life will never find
A Cross between the two is what can make
    The sacrifice of self an act of Reason:
    To love the Lord your God with all your mind.

The Conversion of Augustine
Commentary, Rom. 13:13

The Voice cried out in answer to his need
     To take the plunge, to be converted now,
     Singing, "*Tolle, lege*, take and read."
For years he'd stumbled over the hard creed
     Of Jesus in the flesh—who could see how?
     But nothing less would answer to his need.
His mother's prayers were destined to succeed
     Through Ambrose' preaching, his own quest, and Thou
     Singing, "*Tolle, lege*, take and read."
"But can you live without us? They would plead—
     His mistresses—as if to disallow
     The Voice that cried in answer to his need.
"Yes! Rather put on Christ who came to bleed
     And make no plans the field of flesh to plow."
     Such was the answer he took up to read.
At last the Hound of Heaven had him treed,
     Weeping, broken, and prepared to bow.
     The Voice cried out in answer to his need,
Singing, "*Tolle, lege*, take and read."

Augustine
Answers a Question with a Question

"*Credo ut intelligam*" — to trust,
    The first step in the quest to understand:
    "How can that be?" the skeptic wants to know.
"To question all traditions that were thrust
    Upon us from the past, and to demand
    Proof: How else are we supposed to grow?"

"Yet don't we have perforce to trust the rules
    Of logic as the evidence is scanned,
    Our senses, and our minds in what they show?
And just where do you think we got those tools?
    I'd like to know."

Codex Sinaiticus
The British Museum, London
(Since Moved to the British Library)

Within a very ordinary case
 Of glass that one might easily have skipped
 There lies the greatest link that lets us trace
 Our faith to the Apostles. Quill pen dipped
So carefully in ink, the scribe, equipped
 With great dexterity, capacious learning,
 What was to him an ancient manuscript,
 And sheets of vellum, wrote. The letters, burning,
Flamed in eye and hand and spirit, yearning
 To shine in other breasts. In close precision
 The columns march toward the future, turning
 The simple strokes and curves to holy vision.
And if we do not wander in the night,
 It's men like this who handed us the light.

The Search

Mighty magister Merlin, *sapiens*,
    Of Arthur's court mysterious counselor, chief,
    In lore more learned than all the sons of men,
    Intimate, he, of water, stone, and leaf;
Moses, who on Mount received the Law;
    Solomon king, *princeps* among the wise;
    Jonah, saved from out great fish's maw;
    Magi of the East, who searched the skies:
Long they sought, but could not understand
    Fully how their Lord had overthrown
    Sin, Death, fell Satan's rule in fallen man
    By making His body the true Philosopher's Stone.
What alchemy that! To touch a human soul
    And there to turn base mettle into gold.

The Lindisfarne Gospels
The British Museum, London
(Since Moved to the British Library)

The monks of Lindisfarne illuminate,
 In brilliant tones of gold and blue and red,
 A text. That beckons us to meditate
On what could lead such men to dedicate
 Such long, painstaking labors to the dead?
 The monks of Lindisfarne illuminate
A lot of things, if we but ruminate
 Enough to follow out the knotted thread.
 "A text that beckons us to meditate
Deserves such honor; so we celebrate
 The truth it teaches us," they might have said,
 The monks of Lindisfarne. "Illuminate
Our hearts, restore our souls, and elevate
 Our minds that we may read the way they read
 This text that beckons us." To meditate
Like that before the Lord might be the gate
 That leads us back to where the flock is fed.
 Thus, monks of Lindisfarne illuminate
All texts that beckon us to meditate.

Exile

Dante knew how salt could be the bread,
    How steep the stair,
    How hard the bed
Within the stranger's house to which he'd fled,
Despite how well intentioned, kind, and fair
    The welcome there.
And I myself have seen, a time or two,
    That puzzled stare,
    Uncomprehending,
    Condescending,
From one you would have thought would have a clue
    Why I pursue
The things for which I seem compelled to care.
    But Dante knew:
We who are Pilgrims must be Strangers here,
Where kindred minds are far between and few.
    That much is clear.

Beatrice

In her smile I knew that I could see
    All the bliss that Heaven keeps in store:
    The stronger God that ruleth over me.
I was but nine years old the day that she
    First dawned on me, unlearned in lover's lore,
    But in her smile I knew that I could see
The beauty that resides in sanctity,
    The joy of the Creator's skill, and more:
    The stronger God who ruleth over me.
When on the street she gave her greeting, free,
    There was no greater boon I could implore
    Than in her smile I knew that I could see.
When I was slandered by an enemy
    And she withheld it, oh, my heart was sore,
    For still the stronger God ruled over me.
And when she died and I was lost, her plea
    For grace retaught me what I should adore.
    For in her smile I knew that I could see
The stronger God who ruleth over me.

The Divine Comedy

Beatrice passed in the street, and sweetly she smiled,
    With no idea of what grace in that smile might inhere,
    No thought of the sheen of Shekinah brought suddenly
        near,
Of what bliss could be based in the face of a nine-year-old child.
Innocent sure she remained of what else had beguiled,
    But instead caught the heart of the boy with a call that was
        clear.
    So she lived. When she died, he was lost in a wilderness
        drear,
In the dark of the Wood by his own lack of vision exiled.

Blocked by the beasts, he would have turned back in despair,
    But his Lady looked down and sent Virgil to serve as a
        guide
    For a journey from those who with death-grips will cling
        to their scars,
To the Saints who the pure, searing Fires are eager to dare,
    To the City of those who, to sin and to self having died,
    Are grateful to circle the Center along with the stars.

What Dante Learned from
Piccarda Dei Donatti

"How is it you, sequestered from the bliss
    Which animates those higher yet above
    Who, like the blessed lady Beatrice,
    Dwell even closer to the Source of Love—
How can it be that you are not disturbed;
    How can you be content to languish here?"
    "And have your passions never once been curbed
    By the power of a greater love? I fear
That you will find it hard to comprehend
    The elemental lessons of this school:
    The grammar of the knee that joys to bend
    Before the stronger god who comes to rule.
Our bliss is full, yet ever will increase,
    For we are His, and His will is our peace."

Just a Glance

Thinking some thought of her own, young Beatrice smiled,
    And it leapt from her lips through the eyes to the heart of
        the boy,
    And that street was the path, strait, narrow, yet rocky and
        wild
    That he never could leave 'til it led him to love and to joy.
Levi sat at the table piled high with the cash
    He'd extorted from neighbors, caressing each coin with a
        finger.
    One look in the eye from the Stranger reduced it to trash,
    And the voice, "Follow me!" stripped away any reason to
        linger.
Peter was caught in his headlong plunge to denial
    By a look from the Prisoner standing in Caiaphas' court
    And the crow of a cock. That little sideshow at the trial
    Led to bitterest tears, then to tears of a different sort.
Dare then to share in the sheer delight of the Dance
    When you're granted to glimpse the glory that gleams
        from the Glance.

Vision

For what did Dante climb the winding stair?
A burning and a piercing Charity
That flamed with geometric clarity—
Not Beatrice, but what she wished to share.
She was the first, but not the Final Vision;
Although her face was what had fueled his flight,
Her purpose was to help him to prepare
'Til, in the deepest bosom of the night,
With certain and inexorable precision,
He saw the Point of unrelenting Light,
Infinitely small—and infinitely bright.

The Shrine of St. Thomas A' Becket
Canterbury Cathedral

A candle burns where once St. Thomas' shrine
    Enclosed the holy blissful martyr's tomb
    Until the eighth King Henry's dark design
    Upon its gold reached out and sealed its doom.
The countryside is littered with the bones
    Of great houses sacred to the Lord.
    Godstowe, Glastonbury gave their stones
    To house and barn, their gold to Henry's hoard.
Now nine and twenty ghostly pilgrims pass
    Close by the candle burning on the floor,
    But, like vision in a misted glass,
    The fade from view and soon are seen no more.
The wind blows through the ruins; Heaven turns;
    The pilgrims pass; the lonely candle burns.

Erasmus and the Egg

"Erasmus laid the egg, and Luther hatched it." -- Sixteenth Century
proverb

*"There has never been a great revelation of the word of God unless He
has first prepared the way by the rise and prosperity of languages and
letters, as though they were John the Baptists."* -- Martin Luther,
Letter to Eoban Hess, 29 March 1523.

> Erasmus, reconnecting with the Greek,
> > Gently cleaned away the soot and grime
> > That had accumulated on the cheek
> > Of Jesus' picture slowly over time.
> Astonished at the portrait, he adored,
> > Enchanted by the vision of that Face,
> > And, editing his Testament, restored
> > The primal Scriptures to their proper place.
> That humanist could not fully grasp the storm
> > He had unleashed, nor fully it condone.
> > The base restored, the message must reform
> > As well: the Way, by Grace through Faith alone.
> The church's wounds were too deep to be patched.
> > Erasmus laid the egg that Luther hatched.

Martin Luther

Can one lone monk be right, and all the rest
    Of Christendom for near a thousand years
    Be wrong? The question brought him close to tears
And troubled Luther sorely, he confessed.
But other problems had to be addressed,
    Like, shall the Gospel reach the waiting ears
    Of people whose good works were in arrears
And had no chance but grace to pass the test?

He meant by that just simply every man
    And thought of men who'd lived by faith before—
    And doubted then his Gospel's truth no more.
With Athanasius *contra mundum*, and
    With John the lone disciple at the Cross
    He clung to Christ and viewed all else as loss.

Three Cities:
A Reformation Triptych

Rome

Stained light slanting through the dusty air
    Pointed to the alcove in the nave
    Where in his silent niche the stone saint stood.
Beneath his cool and quiet marble stare
    Passed countless pilgrims marching to the grave;
    He never thought to do them any good.

The contrast, sharp as flesh stripped bare to bone:
    The bone-white marble, impotent to save,
    The flesh flowing past in hopes it would,
Stained red where in his silent niche the stone
    Saint stood.

Wittenberg

Four nails driven deep into the door:
    "The coin into the coffer springs no soul."
    Then, "I can do no other; here I stand."
Because he'd plumbed the Gospel to its core,
    The true treasure of the Church, extolled
    God's grace—for this he had his teaching banned,

Himself, too. In the Wartburg hid for fear,
    Translated Scripture, preached like thunder, told
    Katie he would, the Pope he wouldn't, and
Roared laughing, "I can do no other; here
    I stand."

Geneva

Luther learned the Gospel in his gut
    And taught that Reason was the Devil's whore.
    Calvin fed his mind upon the Book
Until, reformed and sanctified, the slut
    Walked saved and singing through the Church's door,
    Where all her former thoughts she clean forsook.

The Lord repaired the eyes of one born blind
    In Scripture, and he did it one time more:
    And fearfully the Devil's kingdom shook
When God fixed Luther's heart and Calvin's mind
    Upon the Book.

Beatitude

Though faced with Pope and Empire, curse and ban,
Luther's captive conscience dared not flinch.
Latimer and Ridley played the man
And lit a lamp that time will never quench.

Athanasius stood against them all.
Cranmer's hand went first into the flame.
Calvin shook beneath the Elders' call:
Blessed are those who suffer for the Name.

Latimer

The more they smothered it, the more it burned
    With courage and unconquerable will,
    A candle that could never be put out:
It was a blazing soul which only yearned
    To sow the seed of light, and then to till
    The soil until the fruit shone all about.

He saw what only men of faith can see:
    "Play the man, and by God's grace we will,"
    He said, the promise burning through his doubt,
"Light such a candle as shall never be
    Put out!"

The Oxford Martyrs

St. Mary the Virgin has a pillar defaced,
    A ledge chipped in the stone on which to rest
    The beam that held the platform where they placed
    The men they meant to martyr. Who'd have guessed
The way the Faith they stubbornly confessed
    Would rise up like a Phoenix from the flames?
    (A few blocks down, a cross still marks its nest.)
    And when those stalwarts stood to hear their names
Read out as heretics, their mortal frames
    Consigned to fiery death, could they have known?
    Did they by faith then hear the Lord proclaim
    Their place among the martyrs 'round His throne?
Latimer and Ridley played the man,
    And Cranmer clasped the fire by the hand.

The Door
Which once Shut the Oxford Martyrs in their Cell, Since Demolished; Preserved in the Tower of St. Michael's, Northgate, Oxford, England

Your heavy timbers, blackened with the years,
    Once shut Her Majesty's prisoners in their cell.
    Your dull thud locked them up with all their fears
    And with the faith that succored them as well.
Did Cranmer wonder, staring at your blank face.
    If everything he'd done had been for naught?
    Did Latimer think, in that dark, closed-in space,
    The flame had flickered out before it caught?
Did Ridley lean his head against the wood
    In mourning at the Word of God refused?
    The prayers you must have heard! Oh, if you could
    Recall for us the form of words they used—
But there you stand against St. Michael's wall,
    Proclaiming, "I was there . . ." and that is all.

The Sonnet

In Petrarch's soul there bloomed a song whose name
    Was Laura, so with laurel wreath the Muse
    Crowned song and singer, and to us the fame
    Of both comes down in lines we cannot use.
But Wyatt and Surrey heard them from afar
    And with bold, though perhaps yet unsure, hands,
    They plucked the laurel, careful not to mar
    Its form and planted it in their own lands.
In that richer soil it grew full green,
    Tended by husbandmen of highest skill
    Who coaxed it into blossoms yet unseen.
    It withers now, but could yet flourish still
Were but one gardener left to carry on
    The work of Sidney, Spenser, Milton, Donne.

The English Sonneteers: A Villanelle

I come to sing the English sonneteers
    (Not worthy, I, to emulate their form).
    Wyatt and Surrey were the pioneers.
For rules our modern bards have only sneers
    And honor Chaos as their highest norm,
    But I will sing the English sonneteers.
Show me the free-verse monolog that cheers
    The heart, a battlefield for love forlorn,
    Like Wyatt and Surrey, just the pioneers!
The dulcet sequences first reached our ears
    From Italy and France, all full of charm,
    But I will sing the English sonneteers.
For when in Shakespeare's time the thing appears
    We see the first rays of a splendid morn:
    Wyatt and Surrey were the pioneers.
The great ones—Spenser, Milton, and their peers—
    Would follow and the highest truths adorn.
    I come to sing the English sonneteers;
Wyatt and Surrey were the pioneers.

To My Predecessors

Their glory has not faded. Though the years
    Have been kind to barbarians, and, worse,
    Have yielded to their hands the realm of verse;
Though students cannot scan; though I have fears
That Keats will cease to be read by my peers
    Except as an assignment and a curse;
    Yet still this melody I will rehearse:
I come to sing the English sonneteers.

Their glory cannot fade! My tongue repeats
    The words with wonder, hour after hour
Of Sidney, Spenser, Shakespeare, Milton, Keats,
    Of Wordsworth, Hopkins — tastes within their bower
Rich viands, cates, and soul-sustaining meats:
    Each line a world of wit compressed to power.

On the Writing of Sonnets

A perfect sonnet must have fourteen lines,
    Ten syllables in each, the evens strong
    (In French, the sonnet uses twelve and shines,
    But twelve in English verse is just too long).
In Italy it rhymes A B B A.
    A B B A again the octave makes.
    The Sextet then has three rhymes which it may
    Arrange diversely when the sonnet breaks.
Elizabethan sonnets break three times,
    Once after every quatrain, just for fun.
    A B A B and so forth run the rhymes.
    You end them with a couplet; here is one:
This sonnet is not great, but it is good,
    A "perfect" sonnet if you've understood.

On Spenserian Stanza
For Two Teachers:
Edmund Spenser and Frances Ewbank.

When Spenser wrote *The Faerie Queene,* he made
  A brand new stanza up in which to frame
  The glorious knights and ladies he portrayed
  Triumphant over villains full of shame.
  Ever different, yet still the same,
  It had to hold up through the spacious land
  Of Faerie from end to end, and flame
  More bright with virtue there than e'er the hand
Of author had achieved, in verses quaint or grand.

Ottava Rima had the flow he needed,
  But seemed in love a lady far too light
  To shadow forth the gallant knights who heeded
  The Code of Maidenhead and served the bright
  And gracious Gloriana truly. Might
  A pensive sonnet cycle then avail?
  But that would never serve to show the flight
  Of narrative events in time. The tale,
It seemed, must then be dight in wholly different mail.

Yet if the two could somehow be combined—
  Could move with supple dignity, but yet
  Be not in short, concise quatrains confined
  Nor have its forward movement always let,
  Caught in the closing couplet's double net;
  And yet still pause for needed contemplation—
  With light impediment, enough to whet
  The reader's appetite for exploration—
Now that would truly be a gallant innovation!

Suppose we take Ottava Rima, add,
　　　To slow its headlong plunge, a single line,
　　　Rhyming with the last, but subtly clad
　　　With just one extra foot to be a sign
　　　Of need to sip with care such heady wine —
　　　So came The Fairie Queene. And there has been
　　　No poem in which the Glory seemed to shine
　　　More brightly since the storied epoch when
The Sweet Singer of Israel wielded the sword and the pen.

And thou, *doctor mihi carissima,*
　　　Who showed me how to look with eyes undim
　　　Upon the bright, the *ars dulcissima*
　　　Of sacred Poesy, and thence to skim
　　　Cream, not of just *aesthesis*, nor of whim,
　　　But of the Truth well imaged forth, displayed,
　　　Filling the cup of wisdom to the brim;
　　　If worthily I now wield Spenser's blade,
The praise is thine, who long hast labored, taught, and prayed.

The Challenge of "The Republic"

Plato banned the Poets from his state,
  Yet said, if one could make a sound defense
  In lilting verse with cogent arguments
That they do more than merely imitate
An imitation and dissimulate,
  He'd take them back again. And ever since
  Our best minds have been trying to convince
His cautious Guardians of their mistake.

Sir Philip Sidney laid a firm foundation
  In his divine "Defense of Poesy":
  The Poet gives us Virtue's exaltation
More strong than History or Philosophy,
  Concretely shows through his imagination
  Not just what is, but more: what ought to be.

Unfaithful

He saw Christ's blood stream through the firmament;
  A drop—a half drop—would have saved his soul,
  But Faust for comfort turned to Lucifer.
The pain it would have cost him to repent
  Was more immediate a threat, all told,
  Than what an hour later he'd incur.

He could not stop the turning of the spheres
  Or even slow the pace at which they rolled.
  So much for power! That had been the spur
To what he, after four and twenty years,
  No longer could defer.

"The Tempest"
The New American Shakespeare Tavern,
Atlanta, Georgia, 5/24/09

He who lacks the wit to tell
Caliban from Ariel
Or perhaps the will to know
Antonio from Prospero

Nonetheless must cast around,
Confined within the Island's bounds,
While the music in the air
Leads him on, he knows not where.

Who would seek a deeper craft
Must break in twain his carven staff.
Who on higher truths would look
Must cast into the deep his book.

Who would free and fully live
Must his enemies forgive.
Thus across the salt-sea foam
Comes the exile sailing home.

Don Quixote

Clouds of knowing, cloven by a sword
    Whose rust gleamed gold with fierce imagination,
    Part before the tall Manchegan lord
    And recombine in threads of contemplation
Of what is and what ought to be. Conflation
    Of all the ancient chroniclers had said
    Of knights and their heroic occupation
    Danced a poignant dance inside his head.
All the virtue about which he'd read
    Must be fleshed out right here beneath the sun.
    If chivalry could die, the world was dead!
    No nobler, sadder deeds were ever done
For any maid in any olden story
    Than those done for La Dulcinea's glory.

Places

"The mind is its own place, and in itself
Can make a heaven of hell, a hell of heaven."
                                    —Milton's Satan

Though God had filled the universe with grace
        And said, "Come all, drink freely of this well,"
        Satan said the mind was its own place.
In lavish Garden meeting face to face,
        The joys of Him all other joys excel,
        For God had filled the universe with grace.
By willed consent His image they deface:
        "Yea, hath God said?" Thus comes the dreadful
                spell:
        So Satan said the mind was its own place,
And needed not Another's good t'embrace,
        And could without that Other stories tell,
        Though God had filled the universe with grace.
"Supplant the given good with just a taste
        Of fruit which godlike knowledge will compel,"
        Satan said. The mind was its own place,
So self-born goods the Good with bad replace
        And call their evil good and heaven hell.
        Though God had filled the universe with grace,
Satan said the mind was its own place.

Bach Suite
A Five Part Invention

I
Prelude

Joining word to pitch and pitch to time,
Sounds line up to flow into the air.
Bach could make whole lines with lines to rhyme,
And move in streams of thought beyond compare.
Christ gave him this grace, to let us hear
His angels' songs with (now!) the fleshly ear.

II
His Philosophy of Composition

Jesu, juva.

"Jesu, joy of man's desiring,"
Both the words and music say;
Notes and syllables conspiring
Stir the spirit in the clay.

"Come, sweet death!" How so? Inspiring
Men and women thus to pray?
"Jesu, joy of man's desiring,"
Both the words and music say.

"Sheep may safely graze," retiring,
Learn the Shepherd to obey.
Notes and syllables conspiring
Stir the spirit in the clay.

Musicologists inquiring
Cannot brush the thought away:

"Jesu, joy of man's desiring,"
Both the words and music say.

"Jesus, help!" he'd write, requiring
Aid on every page. Today,
Notes and syllables conspiring
Stir the spirit in the clay.

Every page he wrote, aspiring,
"God's alone the glory! May
Jesu, joy of man's desiring,
Be what words and music say."

Just aesthetically admiring
Misses what he would convey:
Jesu, joy of man's desiring,
Stirs the spirit in the clay.

"Jesu, joy of man's desiring,"
Both the words and music say;
Notes and syllables conspiring
Stir the spirit in the clay--
Drive the dark of doubt away.

Soli Deo gloria.

III
Toccata and Fugue in D Minor

Voices shifting like tectonic plates
Send tremors through the whole created order.
Destruction unavoidable awaits.
Can even Bach provide sufficient mortar
To hold this piece together? Notes that border

On madness lead us on toward confusion.
> Then one pitch changes,
> Rearranges
The structure: out of nowhere! Resolution.

IV
Sinfonia to Cantata 29

They say Beethoven wrote an ode to Joy.
> But ne'er fermented a more heady wine
> For comely revelry and celebration
Than Bach served in this piece without alloy:
> "The Sinfonia to Cantata Twenty Nine."
> In organ voices or full orchestration,

The pulsing brasses and the dancing reeds
> Are vying each the other to outshine
> In sheer exuberance of exaltation
Which leaves behind, when all the sound recedes,
> Soul's elevation.

V
Fugue in G Minor, "The Little"

From the initial statement of the theme
> Whose first three pitches rivet our attention
> Upon a coast that cries to be explored,
We glide like pilgrims sailing through a dream.
> Beyond the compass of our comprehension,
> Each voice adds meaning as it comes aboard.

So, wafted on, we sense it coming near,
> Too much like Fate to be our own invention:
> We're exiles drawn unerringly toward

Our home, who recognize it when we hear
    The final chord.

Handel's Messiah
Premiered, Dublin, 1742

The pious found a way to be offended:
    God's Word sung in a public Music Hall!
    It truly was a venue to appall,
Incapable of being comprehended.
Why, vulgar entertainments there were vended,
    With doors thrown open wide to one and all.
    To mix the Gospel with such folderol?
An error that could hardly be amended.

And what would these blasphemers think of next,
    So careless of the Church's reputation?
    Why not associate with sinners? Why,
You might as well proclaim the Sacred Text
    Of God's pure Kingdom and His great salvation
    Out on a hillside underneath the sky.

A Polemic
On the Origins of Post-Modern Criticism
For David Hume

(The radical Empiricism of the Endarkenment entails treating the Good as an abstraction, rejecting Truth for fact, and reducing the Beautiful to a subjective response. Thus it undercuts the *docere* of Literature, leaving us only with a truncated *diligere*. This epistemology applied to Art can only lead to Aestheticism, which inevitably degenerates into Structuralism, Post-Structuralism, and Deconstruction. Once the actual Values of the Sages have thus been destroyed, they can now be replaced with Marxism, Feminism, Freudianism, or whatever other Ism we wish to impose on Texts left defenseless by the death of Truth. To get beyond this impasse, we must abandon the skeptical philosophy that produced it as question-begging Nonsense.)

> That skeptic, David Hume,
> Gained philosophic fame
> Committing to the fume
> Of metaphoric flame
> Whole libraries of pages
> By metaphysic sages.
>
> Unless it could be measured
> By his empiric wit,
> It never could be treasured,
> And so, away with it!
> Mere sophistry, illusion,
> Divinity (!), confusion.

Augustine and Aquinas,
Isaiah, Moses, Paul,
Nothing but a minus;
Better burn them all:
The penalty for treason
Against enlightened "Reason."

Erasmus, Calvin, Luther,
Dante, Milton, Spenser:
What could be uncouther,
More worthy of a censor?
Life seen through the prism
Of rank empiricism.

To keep them as purveyors
Of just imagination
Is but to be betrayers
Of all their conversation:
Dead, white, oppressive pigs
For mere aesthetic prigs.

Good critics can't arise
From bad philosophy.
It should be no surprise
That we have come to be
Despisers of the True —
Of Goodness, Beauty, too.

If only what the senses
Can see or smell or feel
Is able to convince us
That it is really real,
How'd the sensation grow
That tells us this is so?

We'd really like to *know*.

Faithfulness

Dr. Johnson would as lief have prayed
  With Kit Smart as with any man alive.
  So when Smart was summarily betrayed
  And sent to an asylum to deprive
  Him of the insane temper which could drive
  A man to kneeling in the public street,
  The Doctor was the first one to arrive.
  What did he care what base tongues might repeat?
It seems they had to pray wherever they could meet.

Quartet

Newton, Cowper, Wesley, Watts
Worked within their garden plots;
Domesticated by their toil
Exotic plants in English soil:
Pungent spices, soothing balms,
Cadences of David's psalms;
Parsley, sage, rosemary, thyme,
Words of God in English rhyme.
Weeded, hoed, the Garden bears
But few of thistles, thorns, or tares--
Rather, carrots, beans, and maize,
Solid sustenance of praise;
Waving grain and curling vine,
Wheat for bread and grapes for wine;
'Most every plant beneath the sun--
But leeks and garlic grew they none.

Much sand now through the glass has spilled;
They lie beneath the ground they tilled.
But still the seeds they sowed abide
And thrive, transplanted far and wide:
Where e'er a congregation sings,
Anew from earth their produce springs.
Such honor still their Lord allots
To Newton, Cowper, Wesley, Watts.

A Rejoinder to Mr. Wordsworth's "Expostulation and Reply" and "The Tables Turned"

Will bids us Nature's students be
And treat book learning with contempt.
We wonder if his poetry
From this fine maxim is exempt?

I think that what we learn from her
Of moral good and ill is fine;
But after all, I must aver,
It's Man that has a mind!

And God, supremely, who doth teach
Truth absolute in Holy Books
In number sixty-six, and each
A guide to help us look

At Nature's pages, there to see
Aright and not be sore confused.
For Arrogance, who tries to be
His own guide is with ease abused.

I do not seek to minimize
That which from Nature we can know;
I only wish to emphasize
We cannot hope to learn it so!

An impulse from a vernal wood
Could never do me half the good
Without long, careful, studious looks
Between the pages of my books.

"Lies" of the Poets

What is this thing, poetic inspiration?
I can write at will a decent line
In any meter you might specify,
But that will guarantee no fermentation
Of wordplay into visionary wine,
No paradoxical, truth-telling "lie."

Free Verse won't do. You have to learn the craft:
That's how you build the altar, after all.
So follow Form, though men should call you daft,
And then stand back and like Elijah call,
And—maybe—you will see the fire fall.

Appomattox

"I'd rather die a thousand deaths," he'd said;
Well, better he should die them than his men.
Though there was nothing left for them to win,
Still at his word they would have fought and bled
(Or starved, more likely—true—but dead is dead).

So Lee, immaculate in his dress grays,
And Grant, unbuttoned, chewing his cigar,
Sat down together there to end the war.
And when they had agreed on every phrase,
They signed it through an inexplicable haze.

And Lee stepped out upon the porch that day
And drove his fist into his open hand
Three times while staring out across the land.
And then, since there was nothing more to say,
He mounted Traveler and rode away.

And now he'd have to face the thin gray lines.
"It's Gen'ral Lee!" With joy they gathered 'round.
He tried to speak, but could not force a sound,
'Til slowly in his face they read the signs
And silence fell beneath the somber pines.

Only those nearby could comprehend
The words, "Superior numbers ...forced to yield . . .
Your horses you may keep to plow your fields . . .
I've done the best I could for you, my friends.
You're heroes all. Farewell." And so it ends:

The last gasp of the South that might have been,
The first breath of the South as she would be,
Beaten, bowed—but with a memory:

The independence that she could not win,
The Lost Cause, and the frailty of men.

The noblest soldier living could not save
Her from the long defeat or from the tears.
It would protect her for a hundred years
From half the vulgar lies with which men pave
The primrose paths that lead but to the grave.

For Lee stepped out upon the porch that day
And drove his fist into his open hand
Three times while staring out across the land.
And then, since there was nothing more to say,
He mounted Traveler and rode away.

To Gerard Manley Hopkins

Daylight's dauphin, wanwood, diamond delves,
Mountain mindcliffs, lightning, eyes of elves,
Finches' wings or falcons', wolfsnow, wet
Weeds' wildness by the burn bank lingering yet,
Thoughts of Scotus, music of Purcell
Ring out likes stones rim-tumbled in a well.
All are lead-golden echoes, all a view
Of Eden Garden, fresh when it was new
Or cursed and cancerous, fell with Adam's fall,
Blasted with Death's dread worst despair—Not all
Is this the tale. Christ did for that he came,
Grace graces: thus He flings out broad his name;
The Spirit broods still, brooded over you.
Your firedint, mark on mind is never through:
Still in your lines He flings it forth anew!

Theodicy

Hopkins knew the Lord was just, yet pled
    The justice of his own request for rain.
    The Psalmist's echoed accents make it plain,
It wasn't the first time such words were said.
Even Jesus wondered as he bled
    Why God had turned His back upon the pain.
    The Spirit's calculus of loss and gain
Cannot be quickly figured in your head.

So when like Job we groan and question why
    And plead our case, but seem to plead in vain,
    We might remember that the Lord's reply
Was simply a refusal to explain,
    And then a pure, white Lamb who lived to die.
    It is enough: We follow in His train.

Horace, Sidney, and Arnold, Looking Down on Earth from Elysium, Scratch Their Heads

The purpose, by delighting thus to teach
      And then by teaching also to delight?
      Nothing but a lame excuse to preach
      Oppressive values—how naïve, how trite!
The good of History and Philosophy,
      The concrete and the abstract, unified?
      A quaint archaic curiosity
      From European White Males who have died.
To see the thing for what it really is,
      To know the best that have been thought and done?
      Merely factual answers for a quiz;
      No more a map for any race we run.
It's how the academic game is played,
      And Goodness, Truth, and Beauty are betrayed.

"Starry Night"
At the High Museum of Art, Atlanta
On Loan from MOMA

He fought the demons with a tube of paint,
    With knife and brush to joust—cut, thrust, and
        parry.
    Each stroke was life or death: to drive and harry
Unceasing the dark foe, for once to faint
Would yield to black despair, the old complaint.
    Rejected artist, preacher, missionary
    Was more rejection than one man could carry.
In a better church, he might have been a saint.

So still the starlight pierces as it swirls
    Above the silent hills and sleeping town
    Behind the cypress writhing in the wind.
Again the heart its fierce defiance hurls,
    In swaths of yellow, blue, and green, and brown
    Carves out one hour of peace before the end.

Lament
On Seeing Kirk Douglas as Vincent Van Gogh
In "A Lust for Life"

To know the hidden cruelty of life
      Takes no misfortune. The most bitter tear
      That moistens human eyes must come from this:
That Goodness grieves like noble Brutus' knife,
      That Beauty aches like Van Gogh's missing ear,
      And Truth can cut like Judas' parting kiss.

Surrounded by acquaintances, alone,
      We seek one comrade who would want to hear
      The cry that echoes in the soul's abyss.
Ah! If such a friend could be one's own —
      That would be bliss.

The Test

Perhaps the toughest test of writing well
    Is one that's hardly ever tried today:
    The daunting challenge of the villanelle.
The devil's in the details, I can tell.
    Six triplets linked and rhyming A B A:
    Is that the toughest test of writing well?
Oh no, there's more. The trick is in the trail
    The repetitions leave along the way.
    That is the challenge of the villanelle.
Each one must feel like fate as they impel
    The reader onward, never let him stray
    From this, the toughest test of writing well.
When Dylan Thomas' father died, the yell
    Could not be stifled in its fierce dismay.
    Alone the challenge of the villanelle
Could hold such anguish to its task, to spell
    Out clearly what the torn heart had to say.
    He passed the toughest test of writing well:
The daunting challenge of the villanelle.

Read Robinson Jeffers

Read Robinson Jeffers and learn to hew
The strong line from thought as hard as stone
With words sharp as chisels, hard as hammers.
Make it sing like wind in twisted cypress,
Waves warring with the granite sea-cliffs.
Make it speak the slow sanity
Of field and wood beneath the winter sky.
Learn to love the world for what it is,
Embracing pain if pain is what is real—
The harder mysticism of the West:
To love the world outside the brain-vault. Seek
The peace that's almost there in solitude.
Read his poetry and learn his madness:
A heart hurt by hawks and not quite healed
By sea-voice, cypress, starlit distances
Between the mountains and mankind's corruption;
Knew the sickness, knew Redeemer Death
The only way to be cleansed, and did not know
It had been died already; saw the wild
God of the world from afar and partly loved him.
Tell his tragedy: never knew him.

A Parable for Demythologizers
To Rudolph Bultmann

"We come with rusty hatchets to chop down
Old Yggdrasil, the mightiest of trees;
We come with buckets full of air to drown
Old Triton, ruler of the seven seas.

For we are Modern Men, the heirs of Time,
And won't be ruled by anything that's gone
Before. So if we think it more sublime
To exorcise Aurora from the dawn,

Then who is there who dares to say us nay?"
And so the desert wind swept through their minds
And found no obstacle placed in its way
To stop the stinging dust, the sand that blinds.

Blistered, parched, and withered, one by one,
They fell beneath the branches of the Tree,
Succumbing to the unrelenting Sun
In cool, green shade beside the roaring Sea.

The Poetry in Little Magazines
(On the Limits of Imagism and Free Verse)

It struggles haphazardly across the page
In images unconnected by sound or sense.
At intervals, a gleam of freshness glints,
An accuracy of sight which could engage—
But it connects with nothing, does not lead
To anything which can be understood.
The Types—the True, the Beautiful, the Good—
Live not in the bare image; it must breed
With Mind until a Vision is engendered:
A Mediator, not a verbal trick,
To bridge the distance to the *Ding an sich*,
For only so can sanity be rendered—
When such a Child is born alive and quick.

Ars Poetica
A Musical Suite in Four Movements

I
Discursus Discordus
(For a Choir of Contemporary Poets)

We are Artists! Thus, we cannot be
Bound to any false conformity
To Nature (or to Grammar, for that matter).
It is enough if we keep up the chatter!
For we are Artists! Therefore, what we say
Has worth intrinsic. Things are just that way.
So if our lines cannot be understood,
Well, we think that is all more to the good
Because by this they seem the more profound,
Whereby out reputations do abound.
Don't worry whether what we say is true,
It's more important that it just be new!
Each emotion in our hearts that flowers
Makes worthwhile reading just because it's ours.
Edification, timeless truth, insight,
Whether our sentiments are wrong or right—
We can't be bothered by such bourgeois fetters,
For we are Great Souls—Artists—Men of Letters!
Dump the raw emotion on the sheet
To make a lyric poem that can't be beat.
Look, look: We have no tune, and yet we sing!
Oh, come and hear. It is the latest thing.

II
Allegro Stupido
(For Editors, Critics, and Teachers of English)

The Modern Poets have just said
Why they want the Muses dead.
Shall we then resist this trend
And seek the Muses' wounds to mend?
Never! And just cause we'll show
In the lines that come below.

All now confess Modernity
The essence is of quality
And Novelty is the greatest good
That can by man be understood.
Words of beauty, verse that rhymes,
Are not suited to the times.
Rhythm and alliteration
Are a vile abomination.
Like the plague, all now do flee
Metaphor and simile.
If the work makes any sense,
It only proves the poet's dense
And is a vain and snobbish prig.
For meaning, then, give not a fig!
Only an archaizing fool
Would break this, our most basic rule.
If any such these words should hear,
Let him mark well, have no fear,
His fair, just punishment will be
Never his work in print to see.
No, let him not ask us to read
Aught with messages to heed.
Fractured prose, thoughts torn asunder,
Fill the readers' hearts with wonder

And leave them with no ground to tell
The road to Heaven from that to Hell;
And sets us free to fill the nation
With any old interpretation,
Immune from being proven wrong
Or right. And thus the Muses' song
Becomes ('tis our firm resolution)
An instrument of prostitution
Designed to keep us (Aren't we clever?)
In our tenured jobs forever!

III
Nolo Tolerare
(Plaintive Chant for the Reading Public)

Poetry is a pastime for
The pedantic scholar and the bore.
My proof for this? It's plain to see
They're not writing anything for me!
For all I care, their poems can rot.
I'm not a fool! I'll buy them not.

Oh, once I thought that Robert Frost
Had shown me something I else had lost
About a snowy woodland eve . . .
But I was wrong. I was deceived.
The English Teacher (who should know
When such things are and are not so)
Said that he had really written
About a Death Wish that had smitten
The poor old man before his time,
And that was why he wrote the rhyme.
I thought he'd given me a sight
Into the mystery of the night —
How Nature's presence, always near

Could suddenly become quite clear,
Life capsuled in one snowy eve . . .
But I was wrong. I was deceived.

And that's not all: this recent "verse"
Is, if it's possible, even worse.
You can't even think you've caught the scent
Of something the poet might have meant.
Well, I have now been burned enough.
I'm thought with all this wretched stuff.
For all I care, their poems can rot.
I'm not a fool! I'll buy them not.

IV
Hymn to the Logos
(For Solo Non-Conformist)

My search for Freedom always led to Form,
    And only there could I find liberty.
    Inside myself, I found a raging storm
    That had to be bound e'er I could be free.
I sought a channel for my energy
    Though which my will could then direct its flow
    That it not splash into eternity
    And dissipate itself, but rather go
Toward some goal. My soul was my own foe
    And often tried to break out, marring all.
    And yet, by God's grace, I have come to know
    Who my Redeemer is, and what my fall.
He it is who harnesses the storm
    And gives, in life and verse, Freedom and Form.

To C. S. Lewis

On the not long past, convulsive day
That Kennedy bled and died,
One far greater went away
And we noted not his passing.
But in other worlds they cried
For Joy and grief and knew that he was gone.

Eerie voices speaking late that night
In dusky Stonehenge, shrouded in the gloom,
Whispered to the stones
That he had gone.
The beavers and the conies passed the word
Excitedly from lip to beastly lip,
And crickets on that night, and all the birds,
Were hushed because they knew
That he had gone.

A tall sorn standing all alone,
Gazing at a distant speck of light,
Procession of singing hrossa in the night,
Pfiffltrigg slowly shaping brittle stone
Fell silent and stood still like graven stone
And were saddened, for they knew that he had gone
And gladdened, for they knew that he was home.
A faun with an umbrella stopped to sniff the air—
Man odor there—
But strangely changed.
And Aslan's roar of Joy bounced off the cliffs,
For Aslan knew,
And Aslan called his name,
And so he came

With clear grey eyes and did not turn away
But strode with steady foot from night to day
And bowed, and Aslan smiled as if to say,
"Well done."

C. S. Lewis: A Life

"You can't get a cup of tea large enough or a book long enough to suit me." C. S. Lewis to Walter Hooper — reported in Hooper's preface to the Lewis collection *Of Other Worlds: Essays and Stories* (NY: Harcourt Brace Jovanovich, 1966), v.

Such a tapestry his mind could weave:
He gave us Puddleglum and Reepicheep!
Yet there were two things he could not conceive:
A book too long, a pot of tea too deep.

He plumbed the deepest caves of human thought;
He climbed the peaks of poetry and song;
Yet never could he find that God had wrought
A cup of tea too large, a book too long.

Each day would dawn to the same set of plans:
Chapel, breakfast, and then what comes next?
The endless quest to satisfy the man's
Voracious appetite for tea and text.

He gave his time, his energy, his love
To pupils, letters, books, and family,
To friends, chores, God — and the fulfillment of
His endless appetite for text and tea.

The Grave of C. S. Lewis
Holy Trinity Church, Headington Quarry, Oxfordshire

There was a marble slab, the evidence
    Of burial, with writing on the stone
    Which said, "Men must endure their going hence."
The mind that had restored my mind to sense
    Was there reduced to elemental bone;
    There was a marble slab, the evidence.
That well of wisdom and of eloquence
    Was now cut back to just one phrase alone,
    Which said, "Men must endure their going hence."
No monument of rich magnificence
    Stood fitting one who had so brightly shone;
    There was a marble slab. The evidence
That plain things have their power to convince
    Was in that simple block with letters strewn
    Which said, "Men must endure their going hence."
The weight of time was focused there, intense
    With wrecked Creation's universal groan:
    There was a marble slab, the evidence,
Which said, "Men must endure their going hence."

Sehnsucht

When the fog obscures the outlines of the trees
    But breaks to show the sharpness of the stars
    And the blood feels sudden chill, although the breeze
    Is warm, and all the old internal scars
From stabbing beauty start to ache anew;
    When mushrooms gather in a fairy ring
    And every twig and grass-blade drips with dew
    And then a whippoorwill begins to sing;
When all the world beside is hushed, awaiting
    The sun as if it were his first arising
    And you discover that, anticipating,
    You've held your breath and find the fact surprising:
Then all the old internal wounds awake.
    The pain is sweet we bear for beauty's sake.

Sehnsucht II

God knows no shame in what He will employ
    To win a wandering sinner back again.
    Thus, C. S. Lewis was surprised by joy.
A childish garden made to be a toy
    Of moss and twigs upon a biscuit tin?
    God knows no shame in what He will employ.
The silly garden helped him to enjoy
    The real ones, made him want to enter in.
    Thus, C. S. Lewis was surprised by joy.
Not Athens (first), Jerusalem, or Troy,
    But Squirrel Nutkin's granary and bin?
    God knows no shame in what He will employ.
When Balder the beautiful was dead, destroyed,
    The voice that cried it came into his ken;
    Thus, C. S. Lewis was surprised by joy.
But pagan legend! Could that be the ploy?
    Somewhere the path to Heaven must begin.
    God knows no shame in what He will employ;
Thus, C. S. Lewis was surprised by joy.

To J. R. R. Tolkien

On a day when Fall's first leaves were flying
And the wind was howling and geese were crying
And clouds were black and the sun was hiding,
Word first came, on dark wings riding.
    "Tolkien is dead,"
    Was all they said,
    And left us crying.

He heard by light of star and moon
The Elven songs and learned their tunes.
He had long walks with them, and talks,
Beneath the swaying trees in June.

Dwarf-mines deeply delved he saw
Where Mithril glittered on the walls
And mighty kings wrought wondrous things
And reigned in hollow, torch-lit halls.

To forests wild and deep he went
And many lives of men he spent
Where leaves of years fall soft like tears,
Listening to the speech of Ents.

In lofty halls of men he sat
Or rustic rooms of bar-man fat;
In hobbit holes, heard stories told
By an old man in a wizard's hat.

With magic words of dark and light
And days of doom and coming night
And magic rings and hoped for spring,
He wrought the record of his sight....

In Beowulf's bold fleet he sailed,
With Gawain the Green Knight beheld;
By Beortnoth's side he stood and cried
And hordes of pagan Danes he felled,
"Will shall be sterner, heart the bolder,
Spirit the greater as our strength fails!'

On a day when Fall's first leaves were flying
And the wind was howling and geese were crying
And clouds were black and the sun was hiding,
Word first came, on dark wings riding.
    "Tolkien is dead,"
    Was all they said,
    And left us crying.

A Glimmer of Hope

When Bilbo Baggins ran off down the road
    Without a hat or pocket handkerchief
    Or even proper time to say, "Good bye,"
Did Smaug, asleep in his usurped abode,
    Dream of Burglars stealing from the Thief?
    Did Sauron shudder without knowing why?

The hobbit, Gandalf later said, was meant
    To find the Ring: a thought to bring relief
    To Frodo's mind when it was asking, "Why?"
Iluvatar had left at least that glint
    For them to spy.

Aragorn
Smelling the Niphredil in Cerin Amroth
Thinketh on Arwen

Thou wert not there by trail or stream
Beneath the green, tree-filtered light;
Thou wert not there but as a dream
    Remembered from the night.

Thou wert not there by stream or trail
But as a vision sweet and fair.
I tried to take thy hand, but failed,
    Clasping only air.

And will I ever know thee as my wife,
Or will the future leave us both behind?
How can this valley be so full of life
Yet feel so empty, lacking only thine?

Thou wert not there by glade or glen
Except as memory and desire
That burns as strongly now as when
    It first sprang into fire.

Thou wert not there by glen or glade
Save as desire and memory:
Memory that will never fade
    While life is left to me

And will I ever know thee as my wife,
To tip each other that sweet cup of wine?
How can this valley be so full of life
Yet feel so empty, lacking only thine?

Full soon the long, hard road of grief and strife
Resumes. For now, that destiny is mine.

Loth Lorien

From silver trunk the golden leaf
Blows through the old abandoned fief,
For Time, the robber and the thief,
Has brought the hidden realm to grief:
     The wonder is withdrawn.
Now far beyond the Western Sea
The merry folk have gone to be
Naught but a fading memory
     In Caras Galadon.

For untold years Galadriel
Did weave her magic and her spell.
Nor warg nor orc nor dragon fell
Could enter the enchanted veil
     Until it was withdrawn.
Now in the once protected Wood
The Evil mingles with the Good—
Foul things that never could have stood
     In Caras Galadon.

Now through the hushed and chilling air
There rings no voice of minstrel fair,
No melody of sweetness rare,
No magic words beyond compare;
     The music is withdrawn.
The happy sound of harper's glee
Sounds only far beyond the Sea.
The rasping raven's symphony
     Fills Caras Galadon.

In Cerin Amroth, Arwen's tomb
Lies hidden in the gathering gloom.
The niphredil no longer bloom.

- 356 -

She sleeps within that narrow room,
 All memory withdrawn.
The sons to Aragorn she bore:
They come to mourn her there no more.
They sleep beneath the marble floor
Of cold and deep Rath Dinen, far
 From Caras Galadon.

A lonely wanderer passes by;
He sees there is no shelter nigh.
The stars are twinkling in the sky.
He groans, and on the ground doth lie
 Within his cloak withdrawn.
The leaves are rustling on high.
It seems to him they softly sigh
A sad lament—he know not why—
 In Caras Galadon.

The Quest Motif
What Lewis and Tolkien Knew,
but Peter Jackson Does Not

Snaking out across the vast expanse
      Of History and Legend lies a trail,
      The footing treacherous, the markings pale,
And peril lies in wait for those who chance
To travel it. But if they can advance,
      And if their luck and courage do not fail,
      They may emerge into a mystic vale
And find the magic realm of fair Romance.

The landscape's always changing. There is no
      Map that can be trusted once you swerve
      Aside; you only compass is your quest.
If, true to friend, implacable to foe,
      You're faithful to the Vision that you serve,
      You'll find that country which the Muse has blessed.

To Clyde S. Kilby

I

I wandered through the silent trees
    Of fair Loth Lorien,
At Cerin-Amroth saw the leaves
    Blow o'er the tomb of Arwen.

I wandered North to Rivendell,
    To Elrond's homely halls,
And watched as evening shadows fell
    On long deserted walls.

Then West I turned, past hill and tree,
    'Til I stood by the shore.
But Cirdan was gone, and elves to the sea
    Down Anduin sail no more.

II

And I have stood as tall as a king
    On a hill top windy and bare
And drunk the air of a Narnian spring
    When no one else was there.

And I have seen Cair Paravel
    And stood by Aslan's Howe,
But where the king was none could tell
    For no one goes there now.

III

And homeward I my feet have turned
    But there I never came,
For in my soul a fire burned
    And "home" was not the same.

And human eyes I seldom find
    Who seem to comprehend
The longing of a pilgrim mind
    For distant Fairie lands.

But when I find such eyes, I call
    The man who owns them "friend."
And together we wander through leafy halls
    In fair Loth Lorien.

The Pilgrim

I would not leave the sunlit stones
That line the streets of Athens town;
But I will search for Hesperus' Isle,
Though in the end I drown.

I would not turn from Caerleon
Nor Byzantium forsake;
But I will seek Broceliande
Though on her rocks my ship should break.

I lose not lightly Rivendell
Nor Misty Mountains' chilly breath;
But I will sail for Numinor
E'n though I sail to death.

Terabithia

It was waiting there
For them to come at last and set the captives free.
The bond of friendship they had come to share:
        That was the key.

Now you must "close your eyes
But keep your mind wide open." That is how to see
The giant troll, the warriors in the skies,
        The castle tree.

Across the river lay
The land you enter by an all too-fragile swing;
A broken heart, the price you have to pay
        To be the king.

A Metaphysical Conceit

Strange things are taught by Christianity:
That God was born to live a human life;
The mystery of the holy Trinity
Reflected by a husband and his wife
When, by becoming one, two are made three.
It is an awesome thing to slowly see
The growth of one whose coming was prepared,
The Scriptures say, from all eternity—
This, as all others. But this one we've shared,
Yes, and will share: the holy mystery
To be a copy of the Trinity.

For Nelle Ferguson

Throughout the week we watched her slip away.
The words lost focus first, and then the eyes;
The ending, when it came, was no surprise.
(The eyes refocused on a brighter day
While we still wrestled with our long good-byes.)
We'd faced it honestly: There were no lies.
Among the last words I was sure she heard,
I read her favorite psalm: the Twenty-Third.
(The words refocused on a brighter day:
No evil feared—the shadow past—the Prize!)

Nelle Ferguson, II

There's something missing when the people sing.
It was the kind of voice that doesn't blend
Too well with others going through the motions.
But when the old hymns started her devotions,
The she would gather all her joy and fling
It forth, not caring if she bucked the trend.
(She learned her piety back in the old-
Time Wesleyan camp meetings, I am told.)
The angels must have looked up with a start
To hear it blend with their celestial art:
If I know anything, I know that Nelle
Went into Heaven with a "shoutin' spell."

Song
Paraphrase: Habakkuk 3:17-19

Though all my friends should fade like the stars from the sky
    Before the dawn,
Like the leaves in June that greet the breeze with a sigh
    But soon are gone
When the Autumn winds blow sharp and cold, and nigh
    The hearth you're drawn
And the winter snows, so deathly still, seem to lie
    A lifetime long.
Though this and worse should be my lot of woe
    Or grief or care,
Though all of joy should be forgot and go
    I know not where,
Though all the streams of time should seem to flow
    Toward despair,
Still this would be my strength and song, to know
    That You are there—
Unchanged since You laid down your life just so
    I could be spared;
Yes this would be my strength and song, just to know
    That You are there.

The Socratic Method at Work
Michael Bauman Teaching Milton

"The first rule: Don't trust anything I say
    (I might be speaking for the Enemy),
    But when Truth calls to you, you must obey."
The student body shuddered in dismay,
    With pens arrested in mid-note, to see
    The first rule: "Don't trust anything I say."
"For there is Truth, though narrow is the Way,
    And few that find it." (But they will be free
    If, when Truth calls to them, they just obey.)
"Do you think that, or is it just O. K.
    Because I said it?" This, persistently.
    The first rule: "Don't trust anything I say."
"And what is Truth? And what the Good? To play
    The game, you have to know the rules—the key—
    So when Truth calls to you, you can obey."
His every wink and word was to convey
    The simple skill of doubting faithfully.
    The first rule: "Don't trust anything I say,
But when Truth calls to you, you must obey."

Thirty Years Later
Gordon Lightfoot in Concert on PBS, Dec., 2000, Compared with his old Record Jacket

It showed the cruel unkindness of the years:
>The hair, once curly, now lay limp and flat;
>The face was gaunt; the knees were stiff with age;
The voice, less supple, slightly ground its gears.
>But I was still enthralled, for all of that,
>By the aging troubadour upon the stage.

Songs of fulfilled or unrequited love;
>Quixote in his saddle as he sat:
>Heroic perseverance of the sage
Still caught in all the bitter sweetness of
>The Muse's rage.

The Undiscovered Country
For Jaime Fredericks, Fellow Explorer

The mind is poised; the fingers grip the pen.
>Ahead, the unexplored expanse of white
>Lies peaceful, undisturbed—invites you in.
>No one can tell what wondrous things you might
Encounter once the journey has begun:
>The hidden chambers of the human heart,
>That labyrinth that is fully known by none,
>Lie perilously open once you start.
Solar systems far beyond our ken;
>Dragons, wizards, elves, and warriors bold;
>The desperate lives of ordinary men;
>All the untold tales that must be told,
And any one might pick you for its Mage!
>The grand adventure of the empty page.

Opening Night
For Jason Franklin and the Staff,
Corinthian Coffee House Ministries
An Evangelistic Outreach of Trinity Fellowship, Toccoa

Headlights through the lattice, shadows flicker,
Mix with smell of java, candle light;
Above the hum of conversation, laughter;
A string band playing on into the night.
The Cross still standing in its central perch
Is the only sign that we are in a church.

The chairs are not in rows, surround the tables;
The pulpit and the altar, moved aside,
Await their restoration Sunday morning;
Meanwhile the Bridegroom searches for His bride.
The shadows flicker, move toward the back
To find the Cross that stands there draped in black.

Good Friday evening stretches on toward Easter.
The church transformed into a coffee house
Breathes an atmosphere soft and romantic:
'Tis thus the holy Bridegroom woos his spouse.
The Cross, amidst the circling lattice-lights,
By Sunday morning will be wearing white.

For Kathryn
(Kathryn Lindskoog, d. 2003)

Her body, helpless, lay upon the bed,
Its life force all contracted to the head.
She had but one hand that she could control,
The feeble servant of a potent soul,
From which came, tapping, one key at a time,
Her thoughts—some controversial, some sublime—
All driven by the need to understand
The Lion of Judah in never-never land.
And now she does. Fans' cheers, the critics' hiss
Fade out; she wakes up to a Lion's kiss.
The once limp legs can run. The race begins:
"My child! Come further up, come further in."

The Logic of Postmodernism

"Logic's nothing but a verbal trick,"
    Post-Modern thinkers often like to claim.
    They work quite hard to make that judgment stick.
All those who don't agree are simply thick,
    Incompetent to play the language game
    Where logic's nothing but a verbal trick.
It's all a plot by Dead White Males to kick
    Non-Westerners and keep them meek and tame?
    Well, that's one way to make their judgment stick.
"Is there a Text in this class?" Don't be quick
    To ask if there's a prof to ask the same,
    For logic's nothing but a verbal trick.
All truth is surreptitious rhetoric,
    For words call only other words by name;
    The will to power makes this judgment stick!
You say it all sounds just a bit too slick?
    Shh! Shh! Don't give the game away—for shame!
    If Logic's nothing but a verbal trick,
What logic then can make that judgment stick?

The Skeptic and the Text

The Skeptic doubts there even is a Text.
    He hides behind the tiny variations
    And will not hear a reasonable narration
Of methods: what comes first and what comes next,
Criteria to leave us unperplexed.
    His questions answered bring him no elation.
    He must not really want illumination;
The truth he claims to seek just leaves him vexed.

The Seeker of the Truth will not be whipped
    So easily. He turns from what is not
To all the rich wine waiting to be sipped,
    So revels in the pleasures of the plot,
The romance of the ancient manuscript,
    The treasure of the tittle and the jot.

Song
For Loreena McKennitt

From a voice as soft as silk, as strong as steel,
A swift melodic stream in which it would be bliss to drown
That soared aloft, then quavered in a Celtic cadence down
To a place below what we can think or feel.

But from that place both thought and feeling rose
To force their furious way back up and into consciousness.
And is this haunting tune a curse, or rather does it bless?
Such painful beauty, comforting, sharp blows!

And then it faded into air to leave
And aching emptiness until it could be heard again:
A longing for a place, a time — we know not where or when,
Which, though we can't remember, yet we grieve.

How can you lose what you have not possessed?
It was a question that the music could not help but pose.
The notes just shrugged and shook their heads as if to say,
"Who knows?"
But he who hears cannot refuse the quest.

A blessing it imposes and a burden it bestows,
And only in the journey is there rest.

The Piper
For Keith DeLaPlane

There's no expressing what the spirit feels
  When nimble fingers dance with tripping tones
  In energetic jigs and rousing reels
  Across the floor created by the drones.
There's no expressing how the blood is stirred
  When that same wail comes pounding in the head
  Which long ago by those fierce men was heard
  Who bled with Wallace or by Bruce were led.
There's no expressing how the soul is braced
  When those old strains start ringing in the ear
  That bear the words of God's amazing grace.
  How sweet the sound that conquers all our fear!
What do we need for such a robust art?
  The strongest lungs; an even stronger heart.

Ubi Sunt?

  Four decades and a half have disappeared;
  They vanished in the twinkling of an eye.
  And now, the three or four that may remain
  Are poised to follow. It is to be feared
  They'll hardly say "Hello" before they fly.
  Some subtly altered circuits in the brain
  Are the only legacy they leave behind:
  It's what they're literally remembered by.
  And even that inheritance would be vain
  If those faint traces vanish with the mind.
  If anything survives, it's understood
  That there are yet some changes that I would
  Accomplish if I can before I die.

The House
After the Divorce

A little shabby. An observant eye
That pried into the corners would no doubt
Find dust and cobwebs. There had been some effort
At cleaning, straightening—clearly by a man
Who thought he had more pressing things to do.
Original artwork: not untalented,
But by no name that you would recognize.
The main impression would have been the books:
Theology, history, poetry, science fiction,
Philosophy, the Middle Ages, art;
The only expensive piece of furniture
A barrister's bookcase that had been restored,
A legacy from his grandparents. On the top,
A bust of Shakespeare stared across the room
At a wood-frame cradled pseudo-antique globe.
You might have called it quaint or curious;
The man who lived there simply called it home.
But that was not the word on which his mind
Dwelt when he would sink back in his chair
After a day at work and let the silence
Settle around him, silence all the softer
For crickets and the ticking of the clock.

Empty.

He reproached himself for the harshness of the word;
He said that it was not completely fair
To a house so full of good and valued things,
A shelter where he was not alien.
Besides, he said, the word was not all bad:
Suspicion, nagging, strife, misunderstanding,
Ill-disguised resentment, blame, rejection,

A stiff, cold blankness and a harsher silence—
A far worse "empty" to be full of that!

Peace.

Why couldn't that word be the one that came?
It had a claim; it had a valid one!
Why should it only be an after-thought,
Sidling in with a reproachful look,
A guest not adequately appreciated?

Because a better "empty" still is empty;
It is not good for man to be alone.

Definitions
Tending to Show that Theology
Is Indeed the Queen of the Sciences

I

Philosopher: a man who tries to shave
With Ockham's Razor by the flickering light
That shines behind his back in Plato's Cave.
He'll know that's what he's doing if he's bright;
He may take Pascal's Wager if he's brave
(*Fides quaerens intellectum*), and he might
Thus feel his chains fall off and leave that place
And know the sunlight full upon his face.

II

Historian: He deals in documents,
And what he cannot find there he invents.
As long as it fits in with and makes sense
Of what we have of solid evidence,
It's called "interpretation," and he prints
It up. In this there is no vain pretence
As long as we can tell the difference.

III

The **Poet** is a wielder of that Word
Which clothes the unformed thought and makes it seen,
Which sings the silent thought and makes it heard,
Which tells us how to say the thing we mean.

Sir Philip Sidney said it long ago
In his divine *Defense of Poesy*:
Philosophy's business is to seek to know
Not just what is, but that which ought to be,
Truth in its very essence, plain and bare
(Though he may leave it hanging in the air);
History can tell us how, below,
The truth has fared and still is apt to fare;
The **Poet**'s language teaches us to care.

IV

The **Theologian** has to be all three:
The logos, the divine **philosophy**
Which was incarnate in our **history**
Must still be fleshed with words to make men see.
The **Theologian** simply has to be
    All three.

Two Essays on Effectual Calling

I

The fire danced upon the hearth;
The shadows leaped across the wall.
The hobbits stared up at the man,
Travel-worn, but strong and tall,
And wondered how far, if at all,
They dared to trust him. Slow and strained
Had been his words, white and strained
His face. They heard of death and fear
And things they had no wish to hear
And doubted not the truth, but yet the man.
Why should this queer wandering stranger
Seek them out to tell of danger?
They knew not what they stood to gain,
But all too well what they could lose.
They did not know — yet it was plain
They'd shortly have to choose.
The shadows flickered on the paneled wood,
And then the Ranger stood . . .

II

The sunlight danced upon the sand,
The breakers leaped across the shore.
The fisherman's heavy, calloused hand
Clenched the net until it tore,
For he was troubled by Prophet's lore.
The stranger spoke of life and death.
His words were like a salty breath
Of sea-wind on a sun-baked day;
The fisherman reddened, looked away,

And doubted not the truth, but yet the man.
Why should this queer wandering stranger
Seek him out to tell of danger?
He knew not what he stood to gain,
Nor clearly what he stood to lose.
He did not know--yet it was plain
He'd shortly have to choose.
"Leave your nets and come!" He heard him say.
The stranger walked away . . .

On Election and Free Will

All night long we'd sat up and debated
If Man is free, or if his will is fated
To choose as it has been predestinated;
Or, if Man is responsible and free
By God's immutable and fixed decree,
Yet God rules all by strict necessity—
How can necessity and freedom mix?
The whole thing left my mind in such a fix
That I went walking, trying to explain
It all, and so got caught out in the rain.

The first drops turned to steam upon the road,
But soon they all came thick and fast, and flowed
Together. It was possible to tell
The precise moment they no long fell
Directly on the pavement with a hiss,
But joined to form a watery abyss
That rushed to pile itself up in a heap
Along the curbs, and soon was ankle-deep.

And all that water had to go downhill
Until it found some river it could fill,
Which in its turn would have to find the sea.
They did not ask advice from you or me
Or stop to talk abstruse theology,
But just went on about their business, free
To be what their own natures bade them be.

The Noetic Effects of Sin

It was too much of reason to expect
      The world's foundations to be excavated
      By efforts of unaided intellect.
Finite mentalities could not reflect
      Ideas so infinite and elevated;
      It was too much of reason to expect.
Still less would so far fallen minds elect
      The Truth; it never could be venerated
      By efforts of unaided intellect.
Still, their attempts could by no means be checked;
      But though they strove and studied and
          debated,
      It was too much of reason to expect.
Each time they thought they knew, their thoughts
      were wrecked;
      Once more the subtle Quarry had evaded
      The efforts of unaided intellect.
So why then would so few of them inspect
      What in the Bible God himself had stated?
      It was too much of reason to expect
From efforts of unaided intellect.

The Noetic Effects of Sin, II

Though Satan threatens always to deceive
And oft the veil seems heavy on my face,
Lord help mine unbelief, for I believe!
I've seen through every subtle wile he weaves
And would with all my heart your truth embrace,
But Satan threatens always to deceive.
The tyranny of sight gives no reprieve,
More garish than the glimmers of your grace;
Lord, help mine unbelief, for I believe.
The evidence is there; I do perceive
It clearly and myself can make the case,
But Satan threatens always to deceive.
The certainty you help me to achieve
Can sometimes disappear without a trace;
Lord, help mine unbelief, for I believe.
It's all so plain! How deeply you must grieve
To see me still in doubting Thomas' place.
Since Satan threatens always to deceive,
Lord, help mine unbelief, for I believe.

Ecclesia
(The Generality, America, Late 20th Century)

Enemies before her would retreat,
Could find no refuge, even in their gates,
Could she but once advance; and yet defeat
Lies heavy on her face. She hesitates,
Ever stumbling over her own feet.
She cannot lift them, cumbered by the weights.
Insane! She thinks herself well clothed and rich—
All but naked, headed for the Ditch.

Ecclesia II
(When It's Working)

Fellow pilgrims following the Way,
Ambassadors who serve the King of kings,
Members of the Body and the Head;
Itinerants who seek a place to stay,
Listening, believing, questioning,
Yearning to enflesh the Truth they've read.
Overcomers through Another's might,
Finders of the Joy that seeking brings,
Givers of their bounty: beggars' Bread;
Owners of white robes and crowns of light
Derived from One who lives but once was dead.

1st Timothy 3:15
The Founding of Trinity Fellowship

Hard the path of men who live alone:
Outcasts, Eliot's Magi with their race
Uncomprehending, staring, blank of face;
Seeking—those who ought to be their own,
Easily the hardest, hard as stone;
Hearts that claim and mouths and hands that trace
Outwardly the elements of Grace—
Lacking life, corruption over bone.
Daring to believe the Message still,
Onward plodding, leaving Hope behind,
Forgetting hunger for the kindred mind.
Grace has not forgotten all its skill:
Onward plodding, shows us in the trip
Delights unlooked for: founds the Fellowship.

Supper of the Lamb together shared;
Useless baggage seen and laid aside;
Prayer from deepest need—the need supplied;
Preaching from the Text—the Text declared;
Odes of ancient praise renewed and aired;
Royal priesthood serving side by side,
Tasks imposed by Scripture not denied;
Old and new, the treasures are prepared;
Flock responding to the Shepherd's fife;
Truth digested into will and heart,
Realized in acts—at least a start;
Unction of the Spirit bringing life;
Together finally, Boaz and Ruth:
House of God and pillar of the Truth.

Practical Ecclesiology
Commentary, 1 Cor. 14:26, Col. 3:16

Each member has a place; each one belongs,
  As seen when, gathered as a congregation,
  They sing their psalms and hymns and holy songs.
Whether two or three or mighty throngs,
  The Lord is in their midst. A priestly nation,
  Each member has a place; each one belongs.
The Lord himself with love eternal longs
  For them; each one by special invitation
  Is singing psalms and hymns and holy songs.
A pincer movement, ministry: the prongs?
  A verse, a prayer, a word of exhortation.
  Each member has a place; each one belongs.
How beautiful the feet, the sandal thongs
  Which go to every tongue and tribe and nation
  Singing psalms and hymns and holy songs.
Spectators passive in their pew? It wrongs
  The vision, suffocates the celebration.
  Each member has a place; each one belongs,
Singing psalms and hymns and holy songs.

Homiletics 101

Nothing less can speak to our condition,
> Not prooftexts, pretexts; we must have the Word:
> There is no power but in exposition.
The Text is captain of the expedition,
> The Apostle's accents are what must be heard,
> For nothing less can speak to our condition.
The finger on the verse, the fair rendition,
> Then, not to brandish, but to thrust, the Sword:
> There is no power but in exposition.
When heralds mind the message and the mission,
> Not feelings only—mind and heart are stirred,
> And nothing less can speak to our condition.
Can mere opinion lead to true contrition
> When bone and marrow splitting's not incurred?
> There is no power but in exposition.
Such splitting, like the atom: in that fission
> The power is unleashed, the Faith conferred.
> For nothing less can speak to our condition;
There is no power but in exposition.

Another Attempt to Explain
the Spiritual Wimpiness of the American Church

Today's translators are a squeamish lot.
 We are not able, by their estimation,
 To handle hard words like propitiation.
Alright, the word is hard; the thing is not?
And do we need to deal with it, or what?
 A simple failure of determination
 To follow to its final destination
The trail left by the tittle and the jot.

Paul did not write for children or for fools
 (Childlike and humble are another thing),
 But those who loved the Lord with all their mind.
When teachers occupy the dunces' stools,
 We mustn't be shocked if their pupils fling
 The meat away to gnaw upon the rind.

The Roots of Anti-Intellectualism
Commentary, 1 Cor. 1:26

When I was a young and foolish boy,
    I thought intelligence a gift so rare
    That all those who were blessed by it would share
The hunger of the mind for thought, the joy
Of battle on the windy plains of Troy,
    The Big Bang, Quarks—the search for what is there,
    The Saint's hope, the Post-Modernist's despair,
Of Hopkins' call: "Have, get before it cloy!"

The church especially would love to trace
    The Father's hand in all He had created.
    It seems that I had underestimated
How far we've let the Enemy deface
    In us the image of the One who made
    In us the very minds we have betrayed.

A short attention span will pad the purse
    Of publishers who ought to be devoted
    To seeing Truth pursued and then promoted.
They take the easy way. And, what is worse,
We justify our treason with a verse:
    "Not many wise," we've quoted and we've quoted;
    "According to the flesh," we've barely noted.
Thus blithely we perpetuate the Curse.

Willing to know the Evil as the Good,
    We bypassed the Instructions on the Tree.
    Not eating from it would have been the key
To all its fruit, if we had only stood.
    We plucked it green, and greedily we ate.
    Now, gorged with garbage, we push back the plate.

Thoughts

Whence comes a reason's power to convince,
     Illuminate the searching intellect
     With sudden serendipity of sense?
No change of chemicals or elements
     Could equal insight, letting us detect
     Whence comes a reason's power to convince.
Electrical impulses give no hints,
     Yield nothing that could lead us to expect
     A sudden serendipity of sense.
A chain of neurons firing boldly prints
     Its trace upon a screen which can't reflect
     Whence comes a reason's power to convince.
By faith we must accept this light that glints.
     The eye can't see itself, cannot inspect
     Its sudden serendipity of sense.
A mystery much like the sacraments
     Whose grace unseen we yet do not reject:
     Whence comes a reason's power to convince?
From sudden serendipity of sense.

Life in Time

They say the present moment's all we know,
  But when? Once we're aware it's come to be,
  It has receded into memory.
Of the present, all we have to show
Is that the past's a record that can grow.
  We cannot hold it; that's our tragedy,
  That all we really have is history,
The sea where all experience must flow.

The future's out there to anticipate;
  The past is there for us to recollect;
  The present, like the sun, can but reflect
In Plato's Cave, where we are chained by fate.
  So memory, though not enough, is yet
  The only thing we finally can get.

The Need for Critical Thinking in the Church

Why is it that the drive to integrate
     Faith and Learning, Heart and Intellect,
     Is treated as a spiritual defect?
When Jesus said the Truth would liberate,
Could he have meant his followers to hate
     The Mind and all its works, or to reject
     Unheard that Truth for fear it might infect?
It is a strange idea to contemplate.

The world is full of charlatans and liars,
     And they can come quite cleverly disguised.
But has your estimate of who conspires
     With them not ever had to be revised?
To love the Lord with all your mind requires
     A certain willingness to be surprised.

Critical Thinking 101

Where can we find the rhetoric of right?
    With every group and issue polarized,
    Our grammar lacks all grace. The logic of light
Is overcome by Faction. Left and Right
    Are both infected; both are compromised,
    Unable to find the rhetoric of right.
"What do they teach them in those schools?" Well might
    The old professor ask, for he still prized
    The grammar of grace and loved the logic of light.
The Truth still stands with eyes both clear and bright,
    But now it seems her message is despised:
    We cannot find the rhetoric of right.
Lady Reason looks upon our plight
    And shakes her head at how we've ostracized
    The grammar of grace and lost the logic of light.
There will be no recovery of sight
    'Til the Spirit of the Age is exorcized.
    Where can we find the rhetoric of right?
Where the grammar of grace leads on to the logic of
    light.

The Rise and Fall of Protestant Fundamentalism

Christ's virgin birth, His deity, His cross,
    His Word, His resurrection, His return:
    Could these be given up without the loss
    Of Christian faith itself? was the concern
Of those first known as "Fundamentalist."
    If their descendants' words have proved uncouth
    As if their mind had closed up like a fist,
    At least they started caring for the Truth.
It's one of mankind's greatest tragedies
    Beyond the power of the tongue to tell,
    This hardening of mental arteries
    Within a movement that began so well.
What they forgot should be like hand in glove:
    Truth is not Truth unless we speak in love.

The Stakes
A Small but Neglected Part

We flash through time and hardly leave a trace.
　　　　If one could somehow capture in a jar
　　　　The final photon of a dying star
That traveled for millennia through space
To end its pilgrimage in such a place,
　　　　And watch it flicker out, alone and far
　　　　From home: a fleeting glimpse of what we are?
Say what we would be were it not for grace.

The lovely things that pass before our eyes
　　　　Would fade as if they'd never even been
As quickly as the mind that holds them dies,
　　　　And we would know that darkness as the end
We travel to. If Christ did not arise,
　　　　We're truly the most miserable of men.

Counterfeit Spirituality
American Evangelicalism in the New Millennium

　　　　A sanctimonious sobriety
　　　　That masquerades as godly discipline;
　　　　A pathological anxiety
　　　　That claims to be a zeal to flee from sin;
　　　　A stupid, stubborn contrariety
　　　　Presenting itself as love of truth and right;
　　　　Ears that itch for notoriety,
　　　　Eyes not strong enough to bear the light:
　　　　We suffer from the sad satiety
　　　　Of *pietas* degraded into "piety."

A Plea
To Certain Evangelical "Worship" Leaders

What We Think

What elicits deepest feeling?
What promotes profoundest praise?
That were worship whole and healing,
That would set our hearts ablaze!

What We Do

So we focus on emotion,
Turn our gaze within ourselves.
But does that foster true devotion,
However deep the sinner delves?

What We Need

Truth, He promised, is what frees us.
Fill our cup then to the brim!
Stand aside and show us Jesus:
Let our eyes be fixed on Him.

African Suite

Kanisa (Luganda):	Church
Mukama (Luganda):	Lord
Mukama yeba si 'bwe! (Luganda):	Praise the Lord.
Chetibwah cha Mukama (Luganda):	Glory to the Lord.
Soli Deo gloria (Latin):	Glory to God alone.
Muzungu (Luganda):	White man

I
South from Brussels

Wondering if we yet had reached the coast
    Of Africa, I looked up from the page
    Of some pretentious academic sage
And down on what I took to be a floor
Of cloud, which in effect had shut the door
    On that enquiry, yet could not assuage
    Another one: since when were cloud-tops beige?
Which puzzled me for just a moment more.

And then it came to me like stinging sand
    On hot winds blowing through the trackless waste:
    Stretched endlessly, some seven miles below,
Rolling like an ocean made of land,
    The dunes of the Sahara moved, embraced
    Escarpment islands like the drifting snow.

II
Kanisa

The voices shout, "*Mukama yeba si' bwe!*"
The drums are pounding, and the bodies sway.
Hands clap, feet shuffle, and a lady's voice

Leads out to set the song; hers is the choice.
She sings a line; the people sing it back
With zeal and harmony. There is no lack
Of joy. The cry, "*Chetibwah cha Mukama!*"
Resounds through the *Kanisa*. Thus the drama
Of worship is played out in Africa.
And we, whose "*Soli Deo Gloria*"
Is more sophisticated, less intense,
Might profitably pick up a couple hints.

III
Celebrity

"*Muzungu!*" cry the children,
And all then run to see
The ghost who walks in perfect health
Although this cannot be.

"Ooh! Ooh! *Muzungu!* How ah *you*?"
"I'm fine," I smile and say.
And then they giggle, hide their faces,
Grin, and run away.

IV
Legacy

"I look out from my camp, and I can see
        The cook-fires of a hundred villages
        Where no one even knows the name of
            Christ."
And I have come to teach theology
        In places where the smoke he saw still is
        Ascending, next to churches that are priced

At Jesus' blood and missionaries' lives
    Who added their own sacrifice to His,
    Since nothing less than that would have
        sufficed.
They packed in coffins, but their work survives:
    The Church of Christ.

V

Village Evangelism

"But I'm a teacher, not an evangelist."
"No, the muzungu *must preach at the crusade. That way, everybody*
    will come."

    The stars shone on the hills of Africa
    And on a sea of eyes that shone in wonder
    At the generator-driven cinema,
    Another sky of stars that spread out under
    The temporary platform we'd erected.
    They'd never seen a video before.
    The younger ones had never once inspected
    A white man. I can't say which held them more
    Enthralled, the flashing images or my skin.
    It was the skin that made them pay attention
    When, once the "Jesus" film was at an end,
    I rose to preach. And now, what new dimension,
    Stranger than moving pictures on a screen
    Or ghost-like skin in health by some strange art
    Could possibly be waiting to be seen?
    Christ crucified and raised; the human heart
        Made clean.

De Futilitate

When I consider how my light is spent,
    Not lost, like Milton's—rather, cast away
    Like pearls before—That's not what I should say.
It is uncharitable, and I repent.
Yet, I have flown across the continent
    For what? To give a paper? To convey
    Thoughts like soldiers thrown into the fray
To conquer, plant their flag, and stake their tent

Defending all that's holy, good, and true.
    And even if the session's well attended,
    They'll do with mine just what I do with theirs:
All good intentions notwithstanding, to
    File it and forget it. Thus is ended
    Another round of boxing with the air.

We Hold These Truths

"We hold these truths to be self evident:
 All men by their Creator are endowed . . ."
 That's what they said—but what could they have meant?
A wall of separation hard as flint
 With crossing traffic strictly disallowed?
 To some, that answer seems self evident.
"No law respecting an establishment"
 Means no state churches, privileged and proud.
 That's what they said, but what could they have meant?
"Endowed"—by whom? And then, the government
 "Ordained"—by whom? The answer, said aloud,
 Was held by them to be self evident.
Their lives and sacred honors they'd have spent
 Before to merely men they would have bowed.
 That's what they said, but what could they have meant?
"Created equal": could that be a hint?
 Too long this sun has hid behind a cloud.
 We hold this truth to be self evident:
The Founding Fathers said just what they meant.

Life

"Life is pain, Princess. Anyone who tells you different is selling something."

—Westley the Farm Boy

It's not so much a matter of amounts.
    When it comes to suffering, all men have their share.
    They weep in taking their first breath of air
And rattle when their last one they renounce;
Between them, troubles wait their turn to pounce.
    Adrift in apathy; driven to despair;
    Insistently continuing to care?
It's what they let it do to them that counts.

Without deep hurt, true beauty can't be born.
    Those who deny this truth have been abused
    By surface prettiness the eye can see.
The real thing's founded in the way we mourn:
    In sorrow felt and bitterness refused,
    In pain transmuted into poetry.

Friendship

The quest is not for love so much as one
 Who cares about the things you care about.
 You serve a King whose other servants doubt
The worth to Him of everything you've done.
And yet, you know the race you try to run
 Is one He called you to, that He holds out
 The prize, though no one cheers along the route;
Still, running all alone is not much fun.

The quest is not for love. But when you find
 Another runner stumbling down the track
 Whose eyes are focused on the self-same end,
Who has a loyal heart, a kindred mind,
 Who falls in stride with you, does not look back—
 Oh, there'll be love alright: you've found a *friend*.

Connecting Flight
Heathrow, July, 2004

The list of things we could not do was hard
    Enough to try the patience of a Job:
    Shakespeare at the reconstructed Globe;
The rhythmic changing of the Palace Guard;
The Tower, residence of the ill-starred;
    St. Paul's, Westminster Abbey, cross and robe;
    The British Museum, endlessly to probe
That monument to manuscript and shard.

A plane that came too late on the first day
    And one that left too early on the next
    Produced a situation that was rife
With disappointment—but what could we say?
    Dr. Johnson would have known why we were
        vexed:
    "A man who's tired of London's tired of life."

The Radcliffe Camera
(Part of the Bodleian Library, Oxford)

The lamp of learning never shone so bright
    As there beneath that artificial sky,
    The dome of the Radcliffe Camera, graced with light.
That soaring weightlessness of blue and white
    Shot through with gold from skylights lifted high:
    The lamp of learning never shone so bright.
Not truly weightless, all that stony height:
    In the crypt, squat, hunkering arches underlie
    The dome of the Radcliffe Camera, graced with light.
There rooted firm, those arches ground their might:
    Theology and letters; that is why
    The lamp of learning never shone so bright.
That weight of learning buried out of sight
    Was what allowed the mind to soar and fly
    In the dome of the Radcliffe Camera, graced with light.
Here one might mount a search for what is right,
    To extricate the true thought from the lie.
    The lamp of learning never shone so bright:
The dome of the Radcliffe Camera, graced with light.

The Thames River Path
From Godstowe Abbey to Port Meadow

Footsteps fair, unfettered, effortless,
    Together fell in an unhurried pace,
    Andante. On soprano was the lark;
For alto, doves; on tenor, with great zest,
    The waterfowl; a bullfrog took the bass:
    An evensong chorale for none to mark

Except the pair whose slowly lingering feet
    Still blessed the path that led to such a place.
    No care could reach those two contented hearts
While that day lasted, perfect and complete
    In the deepening dark.

The Trout: An Elegy

You cross Port Meadow and its bridge and turn
Right along the river path beside
The Thames, its waterfowl, its reed and fern,
Its wharfs where many a quaint houseboat is tied.
A mallard banks in with its long, slow glide
As you walk on past grazing cow and hare
And swallows gathering in the summer air.

On past the Binsey Poplars, now regrown,
And Godstowe Abbey, shedding as you go
Modernity. The modern clothes alone
On those you meet, the only way you know
It's not a hundred years or more ago.
The place this feeling reached its height had been
The Trout, the ancient English country inn

Just past the ruins of the Abbey. There
The river drifted past so peacefully
You'd nurse your pint or munch your homely fare
Hardly noting electricity
And plumbing, added unobtrusively,
Improvements not permitted to upstage
The old inn's kinship with a former age.

A peacock might come strolling past your table
Out on the patio beside the stream
As if from some old and heraldic fable.
Alas! The old pub's faded like a dream,
The victim of some modern business scheme
From some head full of numbers and equations:
A restaurant requiring reservations!

Sitting there before, you did not doubt
That any moment you might chance to spy
Izaak Walton with a mess of trout
As if four hundred years had not gone by.
I could not help but heave a bitter sigh
To think the centuries could not outlast
The feather of the swan that floated past.

The Romance of England

The mere names: Glastonbury, Stow-on-Wold,
    Stratford-upon-Avon, Oxford, Wells;
        The landscapes: heath and moor, the Yorkshire
           dales,
Ancient forest, hedgerow, field and fold;
The churches: even the most obscure will hold
    Some unexpected treasure—peal of bells
    Forevermore cascading down the scales,
In stone and glass, the ancient Story told.

And then the ruins: Stonehenge, Dead Man's Wall,
    Godstowe Abbey, Whitby, Lindisfarne,
    Or churches whole but empty (that should warn
Us of our own potential for a fall)—
    For all the world contains no richer place
    In history of concentrated grace.

Rending

Missed step—crunch of concrete—searing pain.
> Oh, no! Oh, God, please no—please, not the knee!
> Oh, God, what have I done? It won't unbend.

By hand I wrench it into place again
> And try to walk. The leg will not agree;
> The desperate try comes quickly to an end,

And down I tumble. I'm supposed to speak
> In twenty minutes! It is not to be.
> Some Purpose I cannot quite apprehend

Has intervened. Alright, then, I am weak.
> That truth can rend.

The Book Table

If they had made the parchment from your skin
> And taken your life-blood to use as ink,
> You hardly could be more invested in
> The book. Passing by without a blink,

The public cannot see it. Have they eyes?
> They must; they do not bump into the table
> Nor jostle one another with surprise.
> Imagine if they knew that they were able

To pick one up at a discounted price,
> Save shipping costs and get it autographed!
> Alas, the sign behind you should suffice
> To tell them that. So take another shaft

Of spear to chest and let your heart's blood pour.
> You'll need it for the next planned book of lore.

Prescription for a Broken Relationship

The Heart has reasons Reason doesn't know.
    If either from the other looks away,
    There is no way the person can be whole.
Though we must always pay the debts we owe
    And Reason has a voice we must obey,
    The Heart has reasons Reason doesn't know.
Though she may sometimes feel like Reason's foe,
    The Heart must turn to him and sweetly say,
    "As enemies, we never can be whole."
On hearing this, he must not gloat or crow,
    But grace with grace and courtesy repay:
    The Heart has reasons Reason doesn't know.
When we have fallen, shattered bones may grow
    Back crooked; they cannot be left that way.
    We have to break them then to make them whole.
The sad condition of the human soul
    Needs nothing less its conflicts to allay.
    The Heart has reasons Reason doesn't know,
And only what is broken can be whole.

Negative Capability

Go to the ancient forest,
And there you will find your heart
Enthroned in a shrine of darkness
From which it can't depart.

Go to the barren desert
Beneath the blazing sky;
You'll find your heart is burning
With a flame that will not die.

Go to the trackless ocean,
And there beneath the waves
You'll find your heart is drowning
In hollow emerald caves.

But go to Mount Golgotha,
Beneath the looming Cross,
And there your heart will fail you,
Born down by grief and loss.

And if Another's pain there
Seems strangely like your own
And your heart cries, "Here I should
Have died, and I alone!"

Then go to the lonely Garden
Beside the graven Tomb,
And wait there in the silence
To abide your doom.

It will come as sharp and sudden
As the whistling of a knife:
To know the Tomb is empty
And your heart is full of life.

Unconditional Election

We should not ask the reason for His choice.
    What answer do we think we're going to get?
    "Oh, I foresaw that you would use your voice
    To vote for Me"? What then? Why, that would let
Us say that we were saved because we had,
    More than the lost, the good sense to believe,
    As if we were in any sense less bad.
    What do we have that we did not receive?
No answer is forthcoming that will flatter,
    No answer that would serve to let us boast.
    Some ground in us for Grace? There's no such matter.
    Stop looking for it. Just become engrossed
In the deep mystery of His smiling Face,
    For which the only reason is His Grace.

ဆဝ Index of Titles α

ᛩ Index of First Lines ᛨ

ɶ Index of Scripture Passages ᦔ
Cited or Alluded To

ᔥ Index of Persons and Places ᔤ

Lantern Hollow Press